Riverby Edition

THE WRITINGS OF
JOHN BURROUGHS

WITH PORTRAITS AND MANY ILLUSTRATIONS

VOLUME XIII

Mr. Burroughs in his Study

THE WRITINGS

OF

JOHN BURROUGHS

XIII

FAR AND NEAR

BOSTON AND NEW YORK
HOUGHTON MIFFLIN COMPANY
The Riverside Press Cambridge

PREFACE

In the preface to " Riverby " I told my readers
that that was probably my last out-door book. But
my life has gone on, my love of nature has continued, my habit of observation has been kept up,
and the combined result is another collection of
papers dealing with the old, inexhaustible, open-
air themes. There may even be another volume in
the course of the following year.

The only part of the present collection that has
not been in print before is the chapter on Jamaica.
The account of the trip to Alaska originally appeared in the first volume of the " Harriman Alaska
Expedition," published by Messrs. Doubleday, Page
& Co. in 1901, where it was profusely illustrated
by text cuts, full-page photogravures, and colored
plates. I am indebted to Mr. Harriman and to the
publishers named for permission to use it in this
collection.

August 1, 1904.

CONTENTS

vii

CONTENTS

LIST OF ILLUSTRATIONS

FAR AND NEAR

FAR AND NEAR

I

IN GREEN ALASKA

CROSSING THE CONTINENT

IT was my good fortune during the summer of 1899 to be one of a party of upwards of forty persons whom E. H. Harriman of New York invited to be his guests on a trip to Alaska. The expedition was known as the Harriman Alaska Expedition, and its object was to combine pleasure with scientific research and exploration. The party embraced a number of college professors, several specialists from the biological and geological surveys of the Government at Washington, two or three well-known artists, as many literary men, a mining expert, and several friends and relatives of Mr. Harriman.

We left New York on the afternoon of May 23, in a special train of palace cars, and took ship at Seattle the last day of the month. All west of the Mississippi was new land to me, and there was a good deal of it. Throughout the prairie region, as

a farmer, I rejoiced in the endless vistas of beautiful fertile farms, all busy with the spring planting,
and reaching from horizon to horizon of our flying
train. As a home-body and lover of the cosy and
picturesque, I recoiled from the bald native farmhouses with their unkempt surroundings, their rude
sheds and black muddy barnyards. As one goes
West, nature is more and more, and man less and
less. In New England one is surprised to see
such busy, thriving towns and such inviting country homes amid a landscape so bleak and barren.
In the West, on the contrary, his surprise is that such
opulence of nature should be attended by such
squalor and makeshift in the farm buildings and
rural villages. Of course the picturesque is not an
element of the Western landscape as it is of the Eastern. The predominant impression is that of utility.
Its beauty is the beauty of utility. One does not
say, what a beautiful view, but, what beautiful
farms ; not, what an attractive home, but, what
a superb field of corn, or wheat, or oats, or barley.
The crops and the herds suggest a bounty and a
fertility that are marvelous, but the habitations
for the most part look starved and impoverished.
The country roads are either merely dusty or black
muddy bands, stretching across the open land without variety and without interest. As one's eye grows
fatigued with the monotony, the thought comes to
him of what terrible homesickness the first settlers

2

on the prairies from New England, New York, or Pennsylvania must have suffered. Their hearts did not take root here. They did not build themselves homes, they built themselves shelters. Their descendants are trying here and there to build homes, trying by tree planting and other devices to give an air of seclusion and domesticity to their dwellings. But the problem is a hard one. Nature here seems to covet the utmost publicity. The farmers must build lower and more rambling houses, cultivate more grassy lanes, plant longer avenues of trees, and not let the disheveled straw-stacks dominate the scene. As children we loved to sit on the laps of our fathers and mothers, and as children of a larger and older growth we love the lap of mother earth, some secluded nook, some cosy corner, where we can nestle and feel the sheltering arm of the near horizon about us.

After one reaches the more arid regions beyond the Rockies, what pitiful farm homes he sees here and there, — a low one-room building made of hewn logs, the joints plastered with mud, a flat mud roof, a forlorn-looking woman with children about her standing in the doorway, a rude canopy of brush or cornstalks upheld by poles for shed and outbuildings ; not a tree, not a shrub near ; a few acres of green irrigated land not far off, but the hills and mountains around bare, brown, and forbidding. We saw hundreds of such homes in Utah,

3

Idaho, and Oregon, and they affected me like a nightmare.

A night's run west of Omaha a change comes over the spirit of nature's dream. We have entered upon that sea of vast rolling plains; agriculture is left behind; these gentle slopes and dimpled valleys are innocent of the plow; herds of grazing cattle and horses are seen here and there; now and then a coyote trots away with feigned indifference from the train, looking like a gray, homeless, sheep-killing shepherd dog ; at long intervals a low hut or cabin, looking very forlorn; sometimes a wagon-track leads away and disappears over the treeless hills. How I wanted to stop the train and run out over those vast grassy billows and touch and taste this unfamiliar nature! Here in the early morning I heard my first western meadowlark. The liquid, gurgling song filtered in through the roar of the rushing train. It was very sweet and novel, and made me wish more than ever to call a halt and gain the wild stillness of the hills and plains, but it contained no suggestion of the meadowlark I knew. I saw also the horned lark and the black and white lark bunting from the car window.

Presently another change comes over the scene: we see the Rockies faint and shadowy in the far distance, their snow-clad summits ghostly and dim; the traveler crosses them on the Union Pacific almost before he is aware of it. He expects a nearer

4

view, but does not get it. Their distant snow-capped
peaks rise up, or bow down, or ride slowly along the
horizon afar off. They seem to elude him; he cannot get near them ; they flee away or cautiously
work around him. At one point we seemed for hours
approaching the Elk Mountains, which stood up
sharp and white against the horizon; but a spell
was upon us, or upon them, for we circled and
circled till we left them behind. A vast treeless
country is a strange spectacle to Eastern eyes. This
absence of trees seems in some way to add to the
youthfulness of the landscape; it is like the face
of a beardless boy. Trees and forests make the
earth look as if it had attained its majority; they
give a touch like that of the mane to the lion or
the beard to the man.

In crossing the continent this youthfulness of the
land, or even its femininity, is at times a marked
feature. The face of the plains in Wyoming suggests our Eastern meadows in early spring, — the
light gray of the stubble, with a tinge of green beneath. All the lines are gentle, all the tints are soft.
The land looks as if it must have fattened innumerable herds. Probably the myriads of buffaloes
grazing here for centuries have left their mark upon
it. The hills are almost as plump and muttony in
places as the South Downs of England.

I recall a fine spectacle on the Laramie plains: a
vast green area, miles and miles in extent, dotted

with thousands of cattle, one of the finest rural pictures I ever saw. It looked like an olive green velvet carpet, so soft and pleasing was it to the eye, and the cattle were disposed singly or in groups as an artist would have placed them. Rising up behind it and finishing the picture was a jagged line of snow-covered mountains. Presently the sagebrush took the place of grass and another change occurred; still the lines of the landscape were flowing and the tints soft. The sagebrush is like the sage of the garden grown woody and aspiring to be a bush three or four feet high. It is the nearest that nature comes to the arboreal beard on these great elevated plains. Shave it away, and the earth beneath is as smooth as a boy's cheek.

Before we get out of Wyoming this youthfulness of nature gives place to mere newness, — raw, turbulent, forbidding, almost chaotic. The landscape suggests the dumping-ground of creation, where all the refuse has been gathered. What one sees at home in a clay-bank by the roadside on a scale of a few feet, he sees here on a scale of hundreds and thousands of feet, — the erosions and the sculpturing of a continent, vast, titanic ; mountain ranges, like newly piled earth from some globe-piercing mine shaft, all furrowed and carved by the elements, as if in yesterday's rainfall. It all has a new, transitory look. Buttes or table mountains stand up here and there like huge earth stumps.

Along Green River one sees where Nature begins to dream of the great canyon of the Colorado. Throughout a vast stretch of country here her one thought seems to be of canyons. You see them on every hand, little and big, — deep, rectangular grooves sunk in the plain, sides perpendicular, bottom level, all the lines sharp and abrupt. All the little dry water-courses are canyons, the depth and breadth being about equal; the streams have no banks, only perpendicular walls. Southward these features become more and more pronounced till the stupendous canyon of the Colorado in Arizona is reached.

On our return in August we struck this formation in the Bad Lands of Utah, where our train was stalled a day and a half by a washout. In the Bad Lands the earth seems to have been flayed alive, — no skin or turf of verdure or vegetable mould anywhere, — all raw and quivering. The country looks as if it might have been the site of enormous brickyards ; over hundreds of square miles the clay seems to have been used up to the depth of fifty or a hundred feet, leaving a floor much worn and grooved by the elements. The mountains have been carved and sliced but yesterday, showing enormous transverse sections. Indeed, never before have I seen the earth so vivisected, anatomized, gashed, — the cuts all fresh, the hills looking as new and red as butcher's meat, the strata almost bleeding. The

7

red and angry torrent of Price River, a mountain
brook of liquid mud near which we lay, was quite
in keeping with the scene. How staid and settled
and old Nature looks in the Atlantic States, with
her clear streams, her rounded hills, her forests, her
lichen-covered rocks, her neutral tints, in contrast
with large sections of the Rocky Mountain region.
In the East the great god Erosion has almost done
his work, — the grading and shaping of the landscape has long since been finished, the seeding and
planting are things of the remote past, — but in this
part of the West it is still the heat of the day with
him; we surprise his forces with shovels and picks
yet in hand, as it were, and the spectacle is strange
indeed and in many ways repellent. In places, the
country looks as if all the railroad forces of the
world might have been turned loose to delve and
rend and pile in some mad, insane carnival and
debauch.

In crossing the Rockies I had my first ride upon
the cowcatcher, or rather upon the bench of the
engine immediately above it. In this position one
gets a much more vivid sense of the perils that en-
compass the flying train than he does from the car
window. The book of fate is rapidly laid bare before him and he can scan every line, while from
his comfortable seat in the car he sees little more
than the margin of the page. From the engine he
reads the future and the immediate. From the car

window he is more occupied with the distant and the past. How rapidly those two slender steel rails do spin beneath us, and how inadequate they seem to sustain and guide this enormous throbbing and roaring monster which we feel laboring and panting at our backs. The rails seem ridiculously small and slender for such a task; surely, they will bend and crumple up or be torn from the ties. The peril seems imminent, and it is some time before one gets over the feeling. During this ride of twenty-five miles we struck two birds — horned larks — and barely missed several mourning doves. A big hawk sat on the ground near the track eating some small animal, probably a ground squirrel. He was startled by our sudden approach, and in flying across the track came so near being hit by the engine that he was frightened into dropping his quarry. Later in the day others of the party rode upon the front of the engine, and each saw birds struck and killed by it. The one ever-present bird across the continent, even in the most desolate places, is the mourning dove. From Indiana to Oregon, at almost any moment, these doves may be seen flying away from the train.

SHOSHONE FALLS AND CANYON

The fourth day from home we reached the great plains of the Snake River in southern Idaho, and stopped at Shoshone to visit the Shoshone Falls.

9

Mr. Harriman had telegraphed ahead to have means of transportation in readiness to take us to the falls, twenty-five miles to the south across the sagebrush plains. Hence when we awoke at Shoshone in the early morning, we found a nondescript collection of horses and vehicles awaiting us, — buggies, buckboards, market wagons, and one old Concord four-horse stage, besides a group of saddle-horses for those who were equal to this mode of travel. The day was clear and cool, and the spirits of the party ran high. That ride over the vast sage-brush plain in the exhilarating air, under the novel conditions and in the early honeymoon of our journey, — who of us can ever forget it? My seat happened to be beside the driver on top of the old stage-coach, and we went swinging and rocking over the plain in the style in which I made my first journey amid the Catskills in my youth. But how tame were the Catskills of memory in comparison with the snow-capped ranges that bounded our horizon fifty or a hundred miles away : to the north the Saw Tooth Range and " Old Soldier," white as a snow-bank ; to the southeast the Goose Creek Range; and to the south the Humboldts, far away in Nevada. Our course lay across what was once a sea of molten lava. Our geologists said that some time in the remote past the crust of the earth here had probably cracked over a wide area, allowing the molten lava to flow up through it, like water through rents in the ice, and inundate thousands of square miles of surface, extending even to the Columbia, three hundred miles distant. This old lava bed is now an undulating sagebrush plain, appearing here and there in broken, jagged outcroppings, or in broad, flat plates like a dark, cracked pavement still in place, though partly hidden under a yellowish brown soil. The road was a crooked one, but fairly good. Its course far ahead was often marked to us by a red line visible here and there upon the dull green plain. Flowers, flowers everywhere under the sagebrush, covered the ground. The effect was as of a rough garment with a thin, many-colored silk lining. Great patches of lupine, then the delicate fresh bloom of a species of phlox, then larkspur, then areas of white, yellow, and purple flowers of many kinds. It is a surprise to Eastern eyes to see a land without turf, yet so dotted with vegetation. It is as if all these things grew in a plowed field, or in the open road; the bare soil is everywhere visible around them. The bunch grass does not make a turf, but grows in scattered tufts like bunches of green bristles. Nothing is crowded. Every shrub and flower has a free space about it. The horsemen and horsewomen careered gayly ahead, or lingered behind, resting and botanizing amid the brush. The dust from the leading vehicles was seen rising up miles in advance. We saw an occasional coyote slink away amid the sagebrush.

11

Dark-eared and dark-tailed gray hares bounded away or eyed us from cover. Horned larks were common, and the sage sparrow, the meadowlark, and other birds were seen and heard.

Shoshone Falls are in Snake River, which later on becomes the Columbia. The river does not flow in a valley like our Eastern rivers, but in walled canyons which it has cut into the lava plain to the depth of nearly a thousand feet. The only sign we could see of it, when ten miles away, was a dark heavy line here and there on the green purple plain, the opposite rim of the great gorge.

Near noon we reached a break, a huge gateway, in the basaltic rocks, and were upon the brink of the canyon itself. It was a sudden vision of elemental grandeur and power opening up at our feet. Our eyes had been reveling in purple distances, in the soft tints of the sagebrush plain, and in the flowers and long, gentle, flowing hills, when suddenly the earth opened and we looked into a rocky chasm nearly a thousand feet deep, with the river and the falls roaring at the bottom of it. The grand, the terrible, the sublime were sprung upon us in a twinkling. The chasm is probably a mile or more broad, with perpendicular sides of toppling columnar lava eight hundred feet high. A roadway, carved out of the avalanches of loose rocks that hang upon the sides of the awful gulf, winds down to the river and to the cable ferry above the falls. Our party, in detached groups, made slow progress down to this ferry, there was so much to arrest and fascinate the attention. The new, strange birds, such as the white-throated swift, the violet-backed swallow ; the strange and beautiful wild flowers in the rocks ; the rocks themselves in towering six-sided columns, the spray from the falls below us rising up over the chasm, — these and other features made us tarry long by the way.

In order to get to the front of the falls and pluck out the heart of the sublimity, the traveler must cross to the south side of the river, at this point less than half a mile wide. Here the shore recedes in broad, irregular terraces, upon one of which stands a comfortable summer hotel. Scaling slippery and perilous rocky points near it, we stood on the very brink of the chasm and took our fill of the awful and the sublime as born of cliff and cataract. We clung to stretched ropes and wires and peered down into the abyss. Elemental displays on such a scale crowd all trivial and personal thoughts out of the mind of the beholder. It is salutary to look upon them occasionally, if only to winnow out of our minds the dust and chaff of the petty affairs of the day, and feel the awe and hush that come over the spirit in the presence of such sublimity.

Shoshone Falls are probably second only to Niagara, — less in volume, but of greater height and far more striking and picturesque in setting. Indeed, they are a sort of double Niagara, one of rocks and one of water, and the beholder hardly knows which is the more impressive. The river above the main fall is split up into several strands by isolated masses of towering rocks; each of these strands ends in a beautiful fall, forty or fifty feet in height; then the several currents unite for the final plunge down a precipice of two hundred and fifty feet. To get a different, and if possible a closer view of the falls, we climbed down the side of the chasm, by means of ladders and footsteps cut in the rock and soil, to the margin of the river below. Here we did homage at the foot of the grand spectacle and gazed upward into its awful face. The canyon below the falls is so broad that the river has an easy egress, hence there is nothing of that terrible agony upon the face of the waters that we see in the gorge below Niagara. Niagara is much the more imposing spectacle. Shoshone is the more ideal and poetic. It is a fall from an abyss into a deeper abyss.

A few miles below the falls are still other wonders in the shape of underground rivers which leap out of huge openings in the side of the canyon, — a subterranean water system cut across by a larger river. The streams that emerge in this dramatic manner are doubtless the same that suddenly take to earth far to the northward. Why they also did not cut canyons in the plain is an interesting problem.

In the trees about the hamlet of Shoshone I first made acquaintance with the house finch, a bird with quivering flight and bright, cheery song. It suggests our purple finch, and seems to be as much of a house and home bird as is the ugly English sparrow. The Arkansas flycatcher also was common here, taking the place of our kingbird.

In Idaho we reach a land presided over by the goddess Irrigation. Here she has made the desert bloom as the rose. We see her servitors even in the streets of large towns, in the shape of great water-wheels turned by the current, out of which they lift water up into troughs that distribute it right and left into orchards and gardens. Here may the dwellers well say with the Psalmist, "I will lift up mine eyes unto the hills, from whence cometh my help."

The Oregon Short Line Railroad takes the general direction of the old Oregon trail along Snake River through Idaho and Oregon. It is a treeless country, save for the hand of man and the water from the hills. Vast patches of the original sage-brush alternate with vineyards and orchards, — orchards of peaches, prunes, and apricots, — or with meadows and grain-fields. Where the irrigating-ditch can be carried, there the earth is clothed with grass or grain or verdure. Baptize the savage sagebrush plain with water and it becomes a Christian orchard and wheatfield. Now we begin to

15

see magpies from the car windows, — twinkling black and white wings and a long-tailed body. Lombardy poplars stand like rows of sentinels around the lonely farmhouses. These trees appear to be the only ones planted in this section. The near-by foothills are of a yellowish earth color, speckled as a thrush's breast with sagebrush. In other places lupine and wild sunflowers cover the land for miles, the latter giving a touch of gold to the hills.

After Snake River escapes from the deep lava canyon of Shoshone Falls, it flows for many miles between level banks, with here and there a slowly turning irrigating-wheel lifting the water up to be emptied into troughs or ditches. Near the boundary between Oregon and Idaho the Snake plunges into the mountains ; plump, full-breasted, tan-colored heights close about it on all sides, now dotted with sagebrush, then lightly touched by the most delicate green, the first tender caress of May. All the lines are feminine and flowing, only here and there a touch of ruggedness as the brown rock crops out. Cover these mountains with turf, and they are almost a copy of the sheep fells and green ranges of northern England. They are marked by the same fullness and softness of outline. For many miles the Snake flows north, through these treeless, rounded, flower-painted, green-veiled mountains, until it enters the terrible canyon between the Seven

Devils and the Wallowas. Reappearing at the mouth of the Clearwater, it bends westerly and cuts another long canyon across the high plateau of eastern Oregon and Washington. It does not traverse any flat country until it finally emerges on the sand plains near its junction with the Columbia.

Our train made a long détour through Oregon and Washington, and put us down at Lewiston in Idaho, that we might have a steamboat ride down Snake River to its mouth in the Columbia. I had somehow got the impression that we should see great forests in Washington and Oregon, but we missed them. They are on the moist Pacific slope west of the Cascade Range. We sailed 150 miles that afternoon down the Snake, amid mountains two thousand or more feet high, as smooth and as treeless as the South Downs of England; very novel, very beautiful, their lower slopes pink in places with a delicate flower called Clarkia, in others blue-purple like the cheek of a plum. I say mountains, but they are only the sides of the huge canyon through which the Snake flows. How the afternoon sun brought out their folds and dimples and clinging, delicate tints! The green of the higher slopes was often like a veil of thin green gauze, dropped upon them. The effects were all new to me, and pleasing beyond words, — wild, aboriginal, yet with such beauty and winsome gentleness and delicacy. The river is nearly half the width of the Hudson, and much

17

more winding. The geologists speculated upon the formation as it was laid bare in places; the botanists upon the wild flowers that painted the shore; the ornithologists upon the birds seen and heard. Swarms of cliff swallows were observed about the basaltic rocks near the water.

There were not many signs of rural life, — here and there low, rude farmhouses on the deltas of land at the mouths of the side gorges, and at least one very large fruit farm on a low, level area on our right. A novel sight was the long wooden and wire wheat chutes for running the wheat down from the farms back on the high mountain tablelands to the river, where the boats could pick it up. They were tokens of a life and fertility quite unseen and unsuspected.

MULTNOMAH FALLS

The ride in the train along the south bank of the Columbia toward Portland, past The Dalles, past the Cascades, past Oneonta Gorge and the Multnomah and Latourelle Falls, is a feast of the beautiful and the sublime, — the most delicate tints and colors of moss and wild flowers setting off the most rugged alpine scenery. In places the railroad embankment is decked with brilliant patches of red and purple flowers, as if garlanded for a festival. Presently the moss-covered rocks are white-aproned with the clear mountain brooks that cascade down their sides from the dark, mantling pines and cedars above. They are the prelude of what we are presently to see, — the gem of all this region, and perhaps the most thrillingly beautiful bit of natural scenery we beheld on the whole trip, — the Multnomah Falls.

The train gave us only five minutes to look at it, but those five minutes were of the most exquisite delight. There, close at hand, but withdrawn into a deep recess in the face of the mountain wall, like a statue in an alcove, stood this vision of beauty and sublimity. How the siren mocked us, and made the few minutes in which we were allowed to view her so tantalizingly brief! Not water, but the spirit of water, of a snow-born mountain torrent, playing and dallying there with wind and gravity, on the face of a vertical, moss-covered, rocky wall six hundred feet high. So ethereal, yet so massive; a combination of a certain coyness and unapproachableness with such elemental grandeur and power. It left nothing to be desired but a day in which to picnic upon the flower-covered carpet of moss at its feet. The brief view warmed me up like a great symphony. It was indeed to the eye what the sweetest and most stirring music is to the ear, — harmony, delicacy, and power. Such an air of repose and completeness about it all ; yes, and of the private and secluded. The nymph was withdrawn into her bower, but had left the door open. This ele-

19

ment of mystery and shyness was afforded by the well-hidden rocky basin into which the water fell, and by the curtain of rock which shut it off from our view. Out of this basin the current emerged near at hand and more familiar in a fall of fifty feet or more, whence it took its way to the river in a clear, rapid stream. It was as if the goddess had re-clothed herself in this hidden rock-screened pool and come forth again in more palpable every-day guise. I hardly expected to see anything in Alaska or anywhere else that would blur or lessen the impression made by those falls, and I did not, and probably never shall.

We had hoped that at Portland and Seattle we should get glimpses of the great mountains — Hood, Baker, Rainier — but we did not ; fog and cloud prevented. A lady living upon the heights at Seattle told me that when a dweller there was out of humor, her neighbors usually excused her by saying, " Well, she has not seen the Olympics this morning." I fancy they are rarely on exhibition to strangers or visitors.

THE INLAND PASSAGE

The chapters of our sea voyage and Alaskan ex-periences properly opened on the afternoon of May 31, when we found our state-rooms in our steamer, the George W. Elder, received our California con-tingent, which included John Muir, and made our final preparations for the trip. The steamer was a large iron ship, specially fitted up for our party. Her coal bunkers were full, and she was provisioned for a two months' cruise. We had hunting parties among us that expected to supply us with venison and bear meat, but to be on the safe side we took aboard eleven fat steers, a flock of sheep, chickens and turkeys, a milch cow, and a span of horses. The horses were to be used to transport the hunters and their traps inland and to pack out the big game. The hold of our ship looked like a farmer's barnyard. We heard the mellow low of the red steer even in the wilds of Bering Sea, but the morning crow of our cockerels was hushed long before that time. And I may here anticipate events so far as to say that the horses proved a superfluity, their only association with game being the two foxskins for which Mr. Harriman traded them at Kadiak. But this was no ignoble ending, as they were choice pelts of the rare and coveted black fox. Besides the live stock just mentioned, an inventory of our equipment would include one steam and two naphtha launches, boats and folding canvas canoes, tents, sleeping-bags, camp outfits, and in fact everything such an expedition could possibly need. Our completed party now numbered over forty persons besides the crew and the officers of the ship (126 persons in all), and embraced college professors from both the Atlantic and Pacific coasts — botanists, zoölogists, geologists, and other specialists, besides artists, photographers, two physicians, one trained nurse, one doctor of divinity, and at least one dreamer.

Dr. Dall was our Alaska specialist, having previously visited the territory thirteen times, and having spent many years there. In John Muir we had an authority on glaciers, and a thorough one; he looked upon them with the affection and the air of proprietorship with which a shepherd looks upon his flock. The Indians used to call him the Great Ice Chief. Dr. Fernow was our professor of forestry and might be called the Great Tree Chief. Then what Professors Emerson, Palache, and Gilbert could not tell us about the geology of the country, or Brewer and Gannett about the climate and physical geography, or Coville and Trelease about the plants, or Ritter and Saunders about the life in the sea, or Merriam about the mammals, or Ridgway and Fisher about the birds, or Elliot about the game-birds, or Devereux about mines, or Grinnell and Dellenbaugh about Indians, it could hardly be worth our while to try to find out.

We were in British waters on June 1st and set foot on British soil at Victoria on the Island of Vancouver. Even the climate is British — mist and a warm slow rain — with dense verdure and thick green turf dotted with the English daisy. Indeed, nature here seems quite as English as does the sober, solidly built town with its fine and imposing Parliament building — all but the birds. I heard the western highhole calling like ours at home; and the russet-backed thrush, the yellow warbler, and the white-crowned sparrow were in song along the woods and brushy fields.

On June 1st, after touching at Victoria, we were fairly launched upon our voyage. Before us was a cruise of several thousand miles, one thousand of which was through probably the finest scenery of the kind in the world that can be viewed from the deck of a ship — the scenery of fiords and mountain-locked bays and arms of the sea. Day after day a panorama unrolls before us with features that might have been gathered from the Highlands of the Hudson, from Lake George, from the Thousand Islands, the Saguenay, and the Rangeley Lakes in Maine, with the addition of towering snow-capped peaks thrown in for a background. The edge of this part of the continent for a thousand miles has been broken into fragments, small and great, as by the stroke of some earth-cracking hammer, and into the openings and channels thus formed the sea flows freely, often at a depth of from one to two thousand feet. It is along these inland ocean highways, through tortuous narrows, up smooth, placid inlets, across broad island-studded gulfs and bays, with now and then the mighty throb of the Pacific felt for an hour or two through some open door in the wall of islands, that our course lay.

For two days Vancouver Island is on our left with hardly a break in its dark spruce forests, covering mountain and vale. On our right is British Columbia, presenting the same endless spruce forests, with peaks of the Coast Range, eight or ten thousand feet high, in the background, and only an occasional sign of human life on shore. I recall a lone farmhouse in a stumpy clearing that drew our eyes. How remote and secluded it looked! The dark forests, with a fringe of dead trees where the pioneer's fire had raged, encompassed it. The grass and grain looked green among the stumps, and near the house, which was a well-built, painted structure, we could see fruit-trees and a garden. There was not much wild life about us; now and then a duck or two, an occasional bald eagle, a small flock of phalaropes, which the sailors call " sea geese," as they sit on the water like miniature geese.

Our first dangerous passage was Seymour Narrows, which we reached at the right stage of the tide. Cautiously the ship felt her way through the contorted currents that surged above the sunken rocks. Fog clouds clung to the white peaks that rose above the dark forests about us and partly veiled them. At times we were so near them that with a glass one could see where little snow-balls had detached themselves and made straight lines down the smooth white surface. It was the 2d of June, but the wind that swept down the channel was as cold as that of an October morning at home. The event of this day was the sunset at half-past eight o'clock. I had often seen as much color and brilliancy in the sky, but never before such depth and richness of blue and purple upon the mountains and upon the water. Where the sun went down the horizon was low, and but a slender black line of forest separated the sky from the water. All above was crimson and orange and gold, and all below, to the right and left, purple laid upon purple until the whole body of the air between us and the mountains in the distance seemed turned to color.

As we go north the scenery becomes more and more like that of the fiords on the coast of Norway, except that the mountains there are mostly deforested. Deep sea-blue water about us, dark spruce and cedar clad and torrent-furrowed mountains rising above us, touched with snow on their summits. Now and then a bald eagle flaps heavily along the mountain-side, or a line of black oyster-catchers skim swiftly over the surface. We see Mount Palmerston on our left, five thousand feet high, covered with a heavy snow mantle in which his rocky bones have worn many holes. The brilliant sun brings out every line and angle.

At noon we stop in a deep cove with a rapid stream coming into the head of it, to give some of our party an hour on shore. While we are waiting for them, two deer appear upon the beach, about a mile distant. They browse around awhile, then disappear in the woods. To the west of us is a striking picture. In the foreground is the sea with a line of low, rounded, dark rocky islands; behind them, far off, a range of blue mountains with a broad band of dun-colored clouds resting upon them; rising above the band of clouds a series of snow-covered peaks, with the sun shining full upon them, probably the highest peaks we have yet seen. The cloud belt cuts off and isolates the peaks and gives them a buoyant airy character. From the dark near-by tree-tufted chain of islands to the white-illuminated peaks, what a wealth of blue and gray tints and tones!

Near nightfall on this second day we begin to feel the great pulse of the Pacific around the head of Vancouver Island, through the broad open door called Queen Charlotte Sound. For three hours the ship rolls as upon the open sea, and to several of us the " subsequent proceedings " that night were void of interest.

In the early morning we pass another open door, Milbank Sound, but are soon in Graham Reach, which is like a larger, wilder Hudson. When we look out of our windows the sun is upon the mountain tops, and the snow much farther down their sides than we have yet seen it.

As we progress, many deep ravines are noted in

vast recesses in the mountains, scooped out by the old glaciers. They are enormous rocky bowls which we imagine hold crystal lakes; foaming streams pour out of them into the channel. Far up, silver threads of water, born of the melting snows, are seen upon the vast faces of the rocks. Some of them course down the tracks of old landslides; others are seen only as they emerge from dark spruces.

The snow upon the mountain tops looks new fallen; our glasses bring out the sharp curling edges of the drifts. Here and there along the shore below are seen the rude huts of trappers and hunters. The eternal spruce and hemlock forests grow monotonous. The many dry, white trunks of dead trees, scattered evenly through the forest, make the mountains look as if a shower of gigantic arrows had fallen upon them from the sky. Gulls, loons, and scoters are seen at long intervals.

Snow avalanches have swept innumerable paths, broad and narrow, down through the spruce forest. Those great glacier basins on our left invite inspection, so we send a party ashore to examine one of them. They do not find the expected lake, but in its stead a sphagnum bog, through which the creek winds its way. Fresh tracks and other signs of deer are seen.

In mid-afternoon we turn into Lowe Inlet, a deep, narrow, mountain-locked arm of the sea on

27

our right, with a salmon cannery at the head of it, and a large, rapid trout stream making a fine waterfall. Here, among the employees of the cannery, we see our first Alaskan Indians and note their large, round, stolid, innocent faces. Here also some of us get our first taste of Alaska woods. In trying to make our way to the falls we are soon up to our necks amid moss, fallen timber, and devil's club. Progress is all but impossible, and those who finally reach the falls do so by withdrawing from the woods and taking to boats. Traversing Alaskan forests must be a trying task even to deer and bears. They have apparently never been purged or thinned by fire — too damp for that — and they are choked with the accumulation of ages. Two or three generations of fallen trees cross one another in all directions amid the rocks, with moss over all like a deep fall of snow, and worse still, thickly planted with devil's club. This is a shrub as high as your head, covered with long sharp spines and with large thorny leaves. It is like a blackberry bush with thorns ten times multiplied. It hedges about these mossy cushions as with the fangs of serpents. One can hardly touch it without being stung. The falls are the outlet of a deep, hidden, enticing valley, with a chain of beautiful lakes, we were told, but our time was too brief to explore it. The winter wren was found here, and the raven, and a species of woodpecker.

METLAKAHTLA

We were not really in Alaskan waters until the next day, June 4th. This was Sunday, and we spent most of the day visiting Metlakahtla, the Indian Mission settlement on Annette Island, where we saw one of the best object lessons to be found on the coast, showing what can be done with the Alaska Indians. Here were a hundred or more comfortable frame houses, some of them of two stories, many of them painted, all of them substantial and in good taste, a large and imposing wooden church, a large school-house, a town hall, and extensive canning establishments, all owned and occupied by seven or eight hundred Tlinkit Indians, who, under the wonderful tutelage of William Duncan, a Scotch missionary, had been brought from a low state of savagery to a really fair state of industrial civilization. The town is only twelve years old, and is situated on a broad expanse of nearly level land at the foot of the mountains. The large stumps and logs on the surface between the houses show how recently the land has been cleared. The earth was covered with a coat of peat, the accumulation of ages of a thick growth of moss. Beneath this the soil was red and friable. We strolled about the numerous streets on broad plank walks that reached from side to side above the rocks and stumps. Many of the houses had gardens where were

29

grown potatoes, turnips, onions, strawberries, raspberries, and currants. The people were clad as well
and in much the same way as those of rural villages
in New York and New England. A large number
of them were gathered upon the wharf when we
landed, their big round faces and black eyes showing
only a quiet, respectful curiosity. We called upon
Mr. Duncan at his house and listened to his racy
and entertaining conversation. His story was full of
interest. At eleven o'clock the church bell was ringing, and the people—men, women, and children, all
neatly and tastefully clad — began to assemble for
their Sunday devotions. Some of the hats of the
younger women looked as if fresh from the hands of
a fashionable city milliner. Many of the older ma-
trons wore silk handkerchiefs of various colors on
their heads. Mr. Duncan preached to his people in
their native tongue, a vague, guttural, featureless
sort of language, it seemed. The organ music and
the singing were quite equal to what one would hear
in any rural church at home. The church was built
by native carpenters out of native woods, and its
large audience room, capable of seating eight or
nine hundred people, was truly rich and beautiful.
Mr. Duncan is really the father of his people. He
stands to them not only for the gospel, but for the
civil law as well. He supervises their business enter-
prises and composes their family quarrels.

The Alaskan Indian is of quite a different race

from the red man as we know him. He is smaller
in stature and lighter in color, and has none of that
look as of rocks and mountains, austere and relent-
less, that our Indians have. He also takes more
kindly to our ways and customs and to our various
manual industries.

In reaching the land of the Indian we had reached
the land of the raven also — few crows, but many
ravens. We saw them upon the beach and around
the wharf long before we landed. In the village they
were everywhere — on the roofs of the houses,
and on the stumps and dooryard fences. Six were
perched upon one of the towers of the church as I
approached. Their calls and croakings and jabber-
ings were in the ear at all times. The raven is a
much more loquacious bird than the crow. His
tongue is seldom still. When he has no fellow to talk
to he talks to himself, and his soliloquy is often full
of really musical notes. In these Alaskan settlements
they appear to act as scavengers, like the buzzards
in the South. Other birds that attracted my attention were the song sparrow, a nest of which with
young I found amid some bushes near one of the
houses, and the russet-backed thrush, which was
flitting about the streets and gardens.

In the afternoon we were steaming over a vast
irregular-shaped body of water — Clarence Straits.
On one side the sky and water met in a long hori-

zontal line. The sun was shining brightly, and the far-off snow-capped mountains rolled up against the sky like thunder-heads. Nearer by were small spruce-tufted islands, and low dark shores. Etolin Island was ahead of us, and Prince of Wales Island on the west. In the evening we saw the most striking sunset of the voyage. We were in just the right place at just the right time. All the conditions and relations of sun, air, water, and mountain were as we would have had them — a scene such as artists try in vain to paint and travelers to describe: towering snow-clad peaks far ahead of us, rising behind dark blue and purple ranges, fold on fold, and all aflame with the setting sun. We looked upon the spectacle through a huge gateway in our front which formed a dark rugged frame to the picture. The solid earth became spiritual and transcendent. Presently another dark gateway opened in the mountains on our right and other transfigured summits — Black Crag, Mt. Whipple, the Pinnacles — came into view, riding slowly along above and behind other blue purple ranges — such depth and softness of tint and shadow below, such glory of flame and gold above ! The ship crept along in the deepening twilight and slowly the flaming peaks turned to neutral gray.

WRANGELL AND JUNEAU

The morning of the 5th dawned clear and cold, like a winter morning in Florida. It found us at Fort

Wrangell, where we spent a few hours on shore looking at totem poles and viewing the shabby old town, while we kept an eye open to the botany and natural history of the place. Our collectors brought in a Steller's jay, a russet-backed thrush, an Oregon junco, a gray fox sparrow, a lutescent warbler, a rufous-backed chickadee with nest and eggs, and a Harris's woodpecker.

At eight o'clock we were off again toward Wrangell Narrows, across the superb Wrangell Bay. At noon we saw Devil's Thumb on our right, a naked shaft over sixteen hundred feet high, rising from a mountain which is over seven thousand feet. It is a thumb of goodly dimensions.

The next day we saw our first glacier, the Patterson, a small affair compared with those we were soon to behold; indeed about the smallest lamb of the flock of Muir's mountain sheep, but interesting to novice eyes. It lies there low in the lap or apron of the mountain, and suggests the fragment of an arrested or congealed river. All the afternoon we sailed under cloudless skies along Frederick Sound, feasting our eyes upon the vast panorama of the encircling mountains. When we tired of this there were the low curving shores and nearer-by heights and the numerous tree-capped islands that seemed floating upon the blue expanse of water. Many whales were seen blowing, their glistening backs emerging from the water, turning slowly like the periphery of a huge wheel.

33

We had reached the land of eagles as well as of ravens. On a low rocky point seven eagles sat in a row on the rocks near the water's edge and regarded us with the indifference of Indian chiefs.

We stopped a day at Juneau, from which point we visited the famous Treadwell mines on Douglas Island. Nearly two thousand tons of quartz rock are crushed daily at these mills, and the roar made by the eight hundred or more stamps, all under one roof, in pulverizing this rock, dwarfs all other rackets I ever heard. Niagara is a soft hum beside it. Never before have I been where the air was torn to tatters and the ear so stunned and overwhelmed as in this mill. If the heavens ever should fall and one were under a roof strong enough to stand the shock, I think the uproar might be something like what we experienced that day. It was not a grand reverberating sound like the sounds of nature, it was simply the most ear-paralyzing noise ever heard within four walls. Heard, I say, though in truth we did not hear it. To hear a thing, there must be some silence; this hubbub was so great and all-pervasive that the auditory nerve was simply bruised into insensibility. The remarkable thing about this mine is the enormous extent of the gold-bearing quartz and its low grade — three or four dollars a ton of rock. And yet the process of extracting the gold has been so cheapened by improved methods and machinery that the investment yields a good profit.

34

IN GREEN ALASKA

All the afternoon we steamed up Lynn Canal over broad, placid waters, shut in by dark smooth-based mountains that end in bare serrated peaks. Glaciers became more and more numerous; one on our right hung high on the brink of a sheer, naked precipice, as if drawing back from the fearful plunge. But plunge it did not and probably never will.

We were soon in sight of a much larger glacier, the Davidson, on our left. It flows out of a deep gorge and almost reaches the inlet. Seen from afar it suggests the side view of a huge white foot with its toe pressing a dark line of forest into the sea.

Before sunset we reached Skagway and landed at the long, high pier (the tides here are sixteen or eighteen feet). The pier was swarming with people. Such a gathering and such curiosity and alertness we had not before seen. Hotel runners flourished their cards and called out the names of their various hostelries before we had touched the dock. Boys greeted us with shouts and comments; women and girls, some of them in bicycle suits, pushed to the front and gazed intently at the strangers. All seemed to be expecting something, friends or news, or some sensational occurrence. No sooner had we touched than the boys swarmed in upon us like ants and began to explore the ship, and were as promptly swept ashore again. Skagway is barely two years old. Born of the

35

gold fever, it is still feverish and excitable. It is on a broad delta of land made by the Skagway River between the mountains, and, it seems to me, is likely at any time by a great flood in the river to be swept into the sea. It began at the stump and probably is still the stumpiest town in the country. Many of the houses stand upon stumps; there are stumps in nearly every dooryard, but the people already speak of the " early times," three years ago.

On the steep, bushy mountain-side near the wharf I heard the melodious note of my first Alaska hermit thrush. It was sweet and pleasing, but not so prolonged and powerful as the song of our hermit.

WHITE PASS

The next day the officials of the Yukon and White Pass Railroad took our party on an excursion to the top of the famous White Pass, twenty-one miles distant. The grade up the mountain is in places over two hundred feet to the mile, and in making the ascent the train climbs about twenty-nine hundred feet. After the road leaves Skagway River its course is along the face of precipitous granite peaks and domes, with long loops around the heads of gorges and chasms; occasionally on trestles over yawning gulfs, but for the most part on a shelf of rock blasted out of the side of the mountain. The train stopped from time to time and allowed us to walk ahead and come face to face with the scene. The terrible and

Skagway

the sublime were on every hand. It was as appalling to look up as to look down; chaos and death below us, impending avalanches of hanging rocks above us. How elemental and cataclysmal it all looked! I felt as if I were seeing for the first time the real granite ribs of the earth; they had been cut into and slivered, and there was no mistake about them. All I had seen before were but scales and warts on the surface by comparison; here were the primal rocks that held the planet together, sweeping up into the clouds and plunging down into the abyss. Over against us on the other side of the chasm we caught glimpses here and there of the "Dead Horse Trail." Among the spruces and along the rocky terraces are said to have perished several thousand horses on this terrible trail. The poor beasts became so weak from lack of food that they slipped on the steep places and plunged over the precipices in sheer desperation, and thus ended their misery.

On the summit we found typical March weather: snow, ice, water, mud, slush, fog, and chill. The fog prevented us from getting a view down toward the Klondike country, six hundred miles away. The British flag and the Stars and Stripes were floating side by side on the provisional boundary line between Alaska and British Columbia, and several Canadian police were on duty there. Even in this bleak spot we found birds nesting or preparing to nest: the pipit, the golden-crowned sparrow, and the rosy finch. The vegetation was mostly moss and lichens and low stunted spruce, the latter so flattened by the snow that one could walk over them.

In keeping with the snow and desolation and general dissolution was the group of hasty, ragged canvas buildings and tents at the railroad terminus, the larger ones belonging to the company, the others for the accommodation of traveling gold-seekers. In one of the larger tents a really good dinner was served our party, through the courtesy of the railroad officials. We saw on the trail a few gold-seekers with their heavy packs; they paused and looked up wistfully at our train.

In ascending the Pass we met a small party of naturalists from the U. S. Biological Survey on their way to the Yukon, the entire length of which they intended traversing in a small boat. We stopped long enough to visit their tent and take a hasty look at the interesting collection of birds and mammals they had already secured here. They have since returned and published a report on the results of their labors.

At the time of our visit the railroad terminus was at the summit of the pass, from which point passengers bound for the Klondike were transported to Lake Bennett by sleighs. The deep snow was melting so rapidly and slumping so badly that the sled-loads of people and grain we saw depart for the Upper Yukon were, we were told, the last to go

White Pass

through before the completion of the railroad to Bennett.

The next day found us in Glacier Bay on our way to the Muir Glacier. Our course was up an arm of the sea, dotted with masses of floating ice, till in the distance we saw the great glacier itself. Its front looked gray and dim there twenty miles away, but in the background the mountains that feed it lifted up vast masses of snow in the afternoon sun. At five o'clock we dropped anchor about two miles from its front, in eighty fathoms of water, abreast of the little cabin on the east shore built by John Muir some years ago. Not till after repeated soundings did we find bottom within reach of our anchor cables. Could the inlet have been emptied of its water for a moment, we should have seen before us a palisade of ice nearly one thousand feet higher and over two miles long, with a turbid river, possibly half a mile wide, boiling up from beneath it. Could we have been here many centuries ago, we should have seen, much farther down the valley, a palisade of ice two or three thousand feet high. Many of these Alaskan glaciers are rapidly melting and are now but the fragments of their former selves. From observations made here twenty years ago by John Muir, it is known that the position of the front of the Muir Glacier at that time was about two miles below its present position, which would indicate a rate of recession of about one mile in ten years.

39

What we saw on that June afternoon was a broken and crumbling wall of ice two hundred and fifty feet high in our front, stretching across the inlet and running down to a low, dirty, crumbling line where it ended on the shore on our left, and where it disappeared behind high gray gravelly banks on our right. The inlet near the glacier was choked with icebergs.

What is that roar or explosion that salutes our ears before our anchor has found bottom? It is the downpour of an enormous mass of ice from the glacier's front, making it for the moment as active as Niagara. Other and still other downpours follow at intervals of a few minutes, with deep explosive sounds and the rising up of great clouds of spray, and we quickly realize that here is indeed a new kind of Niagara, a cataract the like of which we have not before seen, a mighty congealed river that discharges into the bay intermittently in ice avalanches that shoot down its own precipitous front. The mass of ice below the water line is vastly greater than that above, and when the upper portions fall away, enormous bergs are liberated and rise up from the bottom. They rise slowly and majestically, like huge monsters of the deep, lifting themselves up to a height of fifty or a hundred feet, the water pouring off them in white sheets. Then they subside again and float away with a huge wave in front. Nothing we had read or heard had pre-

40

pared us for the color of the ice, especially of the newly exposed parts and of the bergs that rose from beneath the water — its deep, almost indigo blue. Huge bergs were floating about that suggested masses of blue vitriol.

As soon as practicable, many of us went ashore in the naphtha launches, and were soon hurrying over the great plateau of sand, gravel, and boulders which the retreating glacier had left, and which forms its vast terminal moraine.

Many of the rocks and stones on the surface were sharp and angular, others were smooth and rounded. These latter had evidently passed as it were through the gizzard of the huge monster, while the others had been carried on its back. A walk of a mile or more brought us much nearer the glacier's front, and standing high on the bank of the moraine we could observe it at our leisure. The roar that followed the discharge of ice from its front constantly suggested the blasting in mines or in railroad cuts. The spray often rose nearly to the top of the glacier. Night and day, summer and winter, this intermittent and explosive discharge of the ice into the inlet goes on and has gone on for centuries. When we awoke in the night we heard its muffled thunder, sometimes so loud as to jar the windows in our staterooms, while the swells caused by the falling and rising masses rocked the ship. Probably few more strange and impressive spectacles than this glacier

41

affords can be found on the continent. It has a curious fascination. Impending cataclysms are in its look. In a moment or two one knows some part of it will topple or slide into the sea. One afternoon during our stay about half a mile of the front fell at once. The swell which it caused brought grief to our photographers who had ventured too near it. Their boat was filled and their plates were destroyed. The downfall from the front is usually a torrent of shattered ice which pours down, simulating water, but at longer intervals enormous solid masses like rocks, topple and plunge. It is then that the great blue bergs rise up from below — born of the depths. The enormous pressure to which their particles have been subjected for many centuries seems to have intensified their color. They have a pristine, elemental look. Their crystals have not seen the light since they fell in snowflakes back amid the mountains generations ago. All this time imprisoned, traveling in darkness, carving the valleys, polishing the rocks, under a weight as of mountains, till at last their deliverance comes with crash and roar, and they are once more free to career in the air and light as dew or rain or cloud, and then again to be drawn into that cycle of transformation and caught and bound once more in glacier chains for another century.

We lingered by the Muir and in adjacent waters five or six days, sending out botanical, zoölogical,

42

and glacial expeditions in various directions; yes, and one hunting party to stir up the bears in Howling Valley. Howling Valley, so named by Muir, is a sort of coat-tail pocket of the great glacier. It lies twenty or more miles from the front, behind the mountains. The hunters started off eagerly on the first afternoon of our arrival, with packers and glistening Winchesters and boxes of ammunition, and we had little doubt that the *genius loci* of Howling Valley would soon change its tune.

While some of us the next afternoon were exploring the eastern half of the glacier, which is a vast prairie-like plain of ice, we saw far off across the dim surface to the north two black specks, then two other black specks, and in due time still other black specks, and the conjecture passed that the hunters were returning, and that the heart of the mystery of Howling Valley had not been plucked out. Our reluctant conjectures proved too true. Just at nightfall the hunters came straggling in, footsore and weary and innocent of blood — soberer if not sadder, hardier if not wiser men. The undertaking involved more than they had bargained for. Their outward course that afternoon lay for a dozen miles or more across the glacier. They had traveled till near midnight and then rested a few hours in their sleeping-bags upon the ice. One may sleep upon the snow in a sleeping-bag, but ice soon makes itself felt in more ways than one. When the cold began to strike up through, the party resumed its march. Very soon they got into snow, which became deeper and deeper as they proceeded. Hidden crevasses made it necessary to rope themselves together, the new hunting-shoes pinched and rubbed, the packs grew heavy, the snow grew deeper, the miles grew longer, and there might not be any bears in Howling Valley after all, — Muir's imagination may have done all the howling, — so, after due deliberation by all hands, it was voted to turn back.

It is much easier in Alaska to bag a glacier than a bear; hence our glacial party, made up of John Muir, Gilbert, and Palache, who set out to explore the head of Glacier Bay, was more successful than the hunters. They found more glaciers than they were looking for. One large glacier of twenty years ago had now become two, not by increasing but by diminishing; the main trunk had disappeared, leaving the two branches in separate valleys. All the glaciers of this bay, four or five in number, were found to have retreated many hundred feet since Muir's first visit, two decades earlier. The explorers were absent from the ship three days on a cruise attended with no little peril.

During the same time an ornithological and botanical party of six or eight men was in camp on Gustavus Peninsula, a long, low, wooded stretch of land twenty miles below Muir Glacier. Here over forty species of birds, including sea birds, were

Glacier Bay

observed and collected. The varied thrush or Oregon robin was common, and its peculiar song or plaint, a long, tapering whistle with a sort of burr in it, led Ridgway a long chase through the woods before he could identify the singer. Other song-birds found were the western robin, the two kinglets, a song sparrow, the Alaska hermit and russet-backed thrushes, the lutescent warbler, the redstart, the Oregon junco, and a western form of the savanna sparrow.

Gustavus Peninsula seems to be a recent deposit of the glaciers, and our experts thought it not much over a century old. The botanists here found a good illustration of the successive steps Nature takes in foresting or reforesting the land, — how she creeps before she walks. The first shrub is a small creeping willow that looks like a kind of "pusley." Then comes a larger willow, less creeping; then two or more other species that become quite large upright bushes; then follow the alders, and with them various herbaceous plants and grasses, till finally the spruce comes in and takes possession of the land. Our collectors found the first generation of trees, none of them over forty years old. Far up the mountain-side, at a height of about two thousand feet, they came to the limit of the younger growth, and found a well-defined line of much older trees, showing that within probably a hundred years an ice sheet two thousand or more feet thick, an older and

larger Muir, had swept down the valley and destroyed the forests.

In the mean time the rest of us spent the days on
the glacier and in the vicinity, walking, sketching,
painting, photographing, dredging, mountain climbing, as our several tastes prompted.

We were in the midst of strange scenes, hard to
render in words : the miles upon miles of moraines
upon either hand, gray, loosely piled, scooped,
plowed, channeled, sifted, from fifty to two hundred
feet high; the sparkling sea water dotted with blue
bergs and loose drift ice ; the towering masses of
almost naked rock, smoothed, carved, rounded,
granite-ribbed, and snow-crowned, that looked down
upon us from both sides of the inlet ; and the cleft,
toppling, staggering front of the great glacier in its
terrible labor-throes stretching before us from shore
to shore.

We saw the world-shaping forces at work ; we
scrambled over plains they had built but yesterday.
We saw them transport enormous rocks and tons
on tons of soil and débris from the distant mountains; we saw the remains of extensive forests they
had engulfed probably within the century, and were
now uncovering again; we saw their turbid rushing
streams loaded with newly ground rocks and soil-
making material; we saw the beginnings of vegetation in the tracks of the retreating glacier ; our
dredgers brought up the first forms of sea life along

46

the shore; we witnessed the formation of the low mounds and ridges and bowl-shaped depressions that so often diversify our landscapes, — all the while with the muffled thunder of the falling bergs in our ears.

We were really in one of the workshops and laboratories of the elder gods, but only in the glacier's front was there present evidence that they were still at work. I wanted to see them opening crevasses in the ice, dropping the soil and rocks they had transported, polishing the mountains, or blocking the streams, but I could not. They seemed to knock off work when we were watching them. One day I climbed up to the shoulder of a huge granite ridge on the west, against which the glacier pressed and over which it broke. Huge masses of ice had recently toppled over, a great fragment of rock hung on the very edge, ready to be deposited upon the ridge, windrows of soil and gravel and boulders were clinging to the margin of the ice, but while I stayed not a pebble moved, all was silence and inertia. And I could look down between the glacier and the polished mountain-side; they were not in contact; the hand of the sculptor was raised, as it were, but he did not strike while I was around. In front of me upon the glacier for many miles was a perfect wilderness of crevasses, the ice was ridged and contorted like an angry sea, but not a sound, not a movement anywhere.

47

Go out on the eastern rim of the glacier, where
for a dozen miles or more one walks upon a nearly
level plain of ice, and if one did not know to the contrary, he would be sure he saw the agency of man all
about him. It is so rare to find Nature working with
such measure and precision. Here, for instance, is a
railroad embankment stretching off across this ice
prairie, — a line of soil, gravel, and boulders, as uniform in width and thickness as if every inch of it had
been carefully measured, — straight, level, three
feet high, and about the width of a single-track road.
The eye follows it till it fades away in the distance.
Parallel with it a few yards away is another line of
soil and gravel more suggestive of a wagon-road,
but with what marvelous evenness is the material
distributed ; it could not have been dumped there
from carts; it must have been sifted out from some
moving vehicle.

Then one comes upon a broad band of rocks and
boulders, several rods in width, the margins perfectly straight and even, pointing away to the distant mountains. All these are medial moraines, —
material gathered from the mountains against which
the ice has ground as it slowly passed, and brought
hither by its resistless onward flow. Some time it
will all be dumped at the end of the glacier, adding
to those vast terminal moraines which form the
gravel plains that flank each side of the inlet. In
looking at these plains and ridges and catching

48

glimpses of the engulfed forests beneath them, one feels as if the mountains must all have been ground down and used up in supplying this world of material. But they have not. Peak after peak many thousand feet high still notches the sky there in the north.

The western part of the Muir Glacier is dead, that is, it is apparently motionless, and no longer discharges bergs from its end. This end, covered with soil and boulders, tapers down to the ground and is easily accessible. Only the larger, more central portion flows and drops bergs into the sea, presenting the phenomenon of a current flowing through a pond, while on each side the water is all but motionless.

Not very long ago the Muir had a large tributary on the west, but owing to its retreating front this limb appears to be cut off and separated from the main ice sheet by a boulder and gravel-strewn ice plain a mile wide. One day three of us spent several hours upon the detached portion which is called the Morse. It is a mighty ice sheet in itself, nearly or quite a mile wide. It is dead or motionless, and is therefore free from crevasses. Its rim comes down to the gravel like a huge turtle shell, and we stepped on it without difficulty. At first it was very steep, but a few minutes' climbing brought us upon its broad, smooth, gently sloping back. The exposed ice weathers rough, and traveling over it is easy.

We found a few old crevasses, many deep depressions or valleys, and several little creeks singing along deep down between blue, vitreous walls; also wells of unknown depth and of strange and wonderful beauty. We came upon a moraine that suggested a tumble-down stone wall, quite as straight and uniform. It soon disappeared beneath the ice, showing what a depth of snow had fallen upon it since it started upon its slow journey from the distant mountains. We pushed up the gentle slope for several miles until the snow began to be over our shoes, when we turned back. I had climbed hills all my life, but never before had I walked upon a hill of ice and stopped to drink at springs that were deep crystal goblets.

The waste of the Morse Glacier is carried off by two large, turbid streams that rush from beneath it, and on their way to the inlet uncover a portion of a buried forest. About this buried forest our doctors did not agree. The timber, mostly spruce, was yet hard and sound, a fact that might almost bring the event within the century. A sheet of gravel nearly two hundred feet thick seems to have been deposited upon it suddenly. The trees, so far as exposed, had all been broken off ten or twelve feet from the ground, by some force coming from the west. In some places the original forest floor was laid bare by the water; the black vegetable mould and decayed moss had a fresh, undisturbed look. Evidently no force had plowed or rubbed over the surface of this ground.

While at the Muir we had some cloud and fog, but no storms, and we had one ideal day. That was Sunday, the 11th of June, a day all sun and sky, — not a cloud or film to dim the vast blue vault, — and warm, even hot, on shore; a day memorable to all of us for its wonderful beauty, and especially so to two of us who spent it on the top of Mt. Wright, nearly three thousand feet above the glacier. It was indeed a day with the gods ; strange gods, the gods of the foreworld, but they had great power over us. The scene we looked upon was for the most part one of desolation, — snow, ice, jagged peaks, naked granite, gray moraines, — but the bright sun and sky over all, the genial warmth and the novelty of the situation, were ample to invest it with a fascinating interest. There was fatigue in crossing the miles of moraine ; there was difficulty in making our way along the sharp crests of high gravel-banks; there was peril in climbing the steep boulder-strewn side of the mountain, but there was exhilaration in every step, and there was glory and inspiration at the top. Under a summer sun, with birds singing and flowers blooming, we looked into the face of winter and set our feet upon the edge of his skirts. But the largeness of the view, the elemental ruggedness, and the solitude as of interstellar space were perhaps what took the deepest hold. It seemed as if the old glacier had been there but yesterday. Granite boulders, round and smooth like enormous eggs, sat poised on the rocks or lay scattered about. A child's hand could have started some of them thundering down the awful precipices. When the Muir Glacier rose to that height, which of course it did in no very remote past, what an engine for carving and polishing the mountains it must have been ! Its moraines of that period — where are they ? Probably along the Pacific coast under hundreds of fathoms of water.

Back upon the summit the snow lay deep, and swept up in a wide sheet to a sharp, inaccessible peak far beyond and above us. The sweet bird voices in this primal solitude were such a surprise and so welcome. There was the piercing plaint of the golden-crowned sparrow, the rich warble of Townsend's fox sparrow, and the sweet strain of the small hermit thrush. The rosy finch was there also, hopping upon the snow, and the pipit or titlark soared and sang in the warm, lucid air above us. This last song was not much for music, but the hovering flight of the bird above these dizzy heights drew the eye strongly. It circled about joyously, calling *chip*, *chip*, *chip*, *chip*, without change of time or tune. Below it a white ptarmigan rose up and wheeled about, uttering a curious hoarse, croaking sound, and dropped back to his mate on the rocks. In keeping with these delicate signs of bird life were the little pink flowers, a species of moss campion, blooming here and there just below the snow-line, and looking to unbotanical eyes like blossoming moss. From the height, Muir Glacier stretched away to the north and soon became a sheet of snow, which swept up to the tops of the chain of mountains that hemmed it in. The eastern half of it, with its earth tinge, looked like a prairie newly plowed and sown and rolled. The seed had been drilled in, and the regular, uniform, straight lines were distinctly visible. Along the western horizon, looking down on the Pacific, the Fairweather Range of mountains stood up clear and sharp, Fairweather itself over fifteen thousand feet high. The snow upon these mountains doubtless in places lay over one hundred feet deep.

Glaciers are formed wherever more snow falls in winter than can melt in summer, and this seems to be the case on all these Alaskan mountains on the Pacific coast. If by a change of climate more snow should fall in the Hudson River valley than could melt in summer, our landscapes would soon be invaded by glaciers from the Catskills. Farther north in Alaska, beyond the reach of the moisture-loaded Pacific air currents, the precipitation is less and there are no glaciers.

SITKA

On the 13th of June we weighed anchor, and after picking up our camping and exploring parties,

steamed away toward Sitka, where we arrived
under dripping skies the next morning. We had
come from air and water streaked with icy currents,
to much warmer and to much moister conditions.
Sitka is said to be one of the rainiest spots on the
coast, but the four days we passed there were not
so bad: sun and cloud and spurts of rain each day,
but no considerable downpour. We came into the
island-studded and mountain-locked harbor from
the north, and saw the town, with its quaint old
government buildings and its line of Indian houses
close to the beach, outlined against a near-by background of steep, high, spruce-covered and snow-
capped mountains, with the white volcanic cone of
Edgecumbe three thousand feet high toward the
open ocean on our right.

People actually live in Sitka from choice, and
seem to find life sweet. There are homes of culture
and refinement there. Governor Brady is a Yale
graduate, and his accomplished wife would shine
in any society. At a reception given us by the
governor, we met teachers from New England and
people who keep in touch with current literature.
A retired naval officer told us he liked the Sitka
climate and life the best of any he had found. He
and his family throve the best there. We spent
the time after the usual manner of tourists: walking about the town, visiting the Indian village,
the museum, the Greek church, going to the Hot

Sitka Harbor

Springs, a few hours' sail to the south, exploring Indian River, a large, ideal trout stream in appearance, making a trip to some near-by mines, and climbing the mountains. It was not a good place for our collectors; there were but few birds, and they were very wild. Our mammal collectors put out one hundred small traps and caught only two mice. I was fortunate enough to see and hear the water ouzel along Indian River, a bird like a big water-colored pebble, with a liquid, bubbling song, caught from the currents about it. Here also I saw the golden-crowned kinglet, the varied thrush, the russet-backed thrush, and the rufous chickadee. Ravens were very common everywhere in the town and about it, and were talking and croaking all the time. Often a solitary bird seemed to be so-liloquizing and repeating over to himself every note he knew. One day a hunting party, with Indian guides and dogs, visited one of the islands in quest of deer; the only deer that fell to their rifles was killed by Mr. Harriman's eldest daughter, Mary.

It was a surprise to see the vast spruce forests about Sitka almost untouched by the axe, except on a small area behind the town. In the forest near the mouth of Indian River I noticed a few huge stumps twelve feet high, as if the axe that felled the trees had been wielded by giants. The cutting had probably been done from raised platforms. Some of the stumps

were very old, doubtless the work of the Russians.
Sitka is very prettily situated; a ring of high, dark,
snow-topped mountains just behind it, and a sparkling bay, dotted with islands, rock-based and tree-
crowned, in its front, with white volcanic cones in
the distance. About the only bit of smooth dirt-road
we saw in Alaska, we walked on here for the distance
of a mile, in going from the town to the park.

IN YAKUTAT BAY

After four warm, humid days at Sitka we turned
our faces for the first time toward the open ocean,
our objective point being Yakutat Bay, a day's run
farther north. The usual Alaska excursion ends at
Sitka, but ours was now only fairly begun. The
Pacific was very good to us, and used us as gently as
an inland lake, there being only a long, low, sleepy
swell that did not disturb the most sensitive. The
next day, Sunday the 18th, was mild and placid.
Far at sea on our left we looked into a world of sunshine, but above us and on our right lay a heavy
blanket of clouds, enveloping and blotting out all
the upper portions of the great Fairweather Range.
We steamed all day a few miles offshore, hoping
that the great peaks, some of them fifteen thousand
to sixteen thousand feet high, would reveal themselves, but they did not. We saw them only from
the waist down, as it were, with their glaciers like
vast white aprons flanked by skirts of spruce forests.

One of these glaciers, La Perouse, came quite down
to the sea, with a front a mile or more long and two
hundred feet high. At one point it had cut into the
edge of the forest, and shoved and piled up the trees
and soil as a heavy vehicle shoves and folds up the
turf. This, of course, showed that quite recently
the glacier had had a period of advance or augmen-
tation, and had encroached upon its banks. We
stopped an hour in front of it and put a party ashore,
but they learned little that could not be divined
from the ship. They found a heavy surf running,
and did not get through it on their return without an
acquaintance with the Pacific more intimate than
agreeable. All day long we were in sight of glaciers,
usually two or three at a time, some of them immense, all the offspring of the great Fairweather
Range. Now and then the back of one some miles
inland would show above a low wooded ridge, a line
of white above an expanse of black, like the crest of
a river about to overflow its banks. One broad ice
slope I recall which, with its dark, straight lines of
moraine dividing it into three equal portions, suggested a side-hill farm in winter with the tops of the
stone walls showing above the snow. It had a
friendly, home look to me.

On the morning of the 19th we were at anchor
in front of the Indian village in Yakutat Bay. This
bay is literally like an arm, a huge arm of the sea,
very broad and heavy at the shoulder, much flexed

at the elbow, where it breaks into the St. Elias
Range, and long and slender in the forearm, which
is thrust through the mountains till it nearly reaches
the sea again. Eight or ten comfortable frame
houses, with a store and post-office, made up the
Indian village known on the map as Yakutat. It sat
low on a wooded point just to one side of the broad
entrance to the bay. There were upwards of a hundred people there, looked after by a Swedish missionary. We soon proceeded up the bay, with the
great Malaspina Glacier on our left, and put off
three hunting and collecting parties, to be absent
from the ship till Thursday. The event of this day
was the view of Mt. St. Elias that was vouchsafed
us for half an hour in the afternoon. The base and
lower ranges had been visible for some time, bathed
in clear sunshine, but a heavy canopy of dun-colored
clouds hung above us, and stretched away toward
the mountain, dropping down there in many cur-
tain-like folds, hiding the peak. But the scene-
shifters were at work; slowly the heavy folds of
clouds that limited our view yielded and were spun
off by the air currents, till at last the veil was com-
pletely rent, and there, in the depths of clear air and
sunshine, the huge mass soared to heaven.

There is sublimity in the sight of a summer
thunder-head with its great white and dun convolu-
tions rising up for miles against the sky, but there is
more in the vision of a jagged mountain crest pier-

cing the blue at even a lesser height. This is partly because it is a much rarer spectacle, but mainly because it is a display of power that takes greater hold of the imagination. That lift heavenward of the solid crust of the earth, that aspiration of the insensate rocks, that effort of the whole range, as it were, to carry one peak into heights where all may not go, — every lower summit seeming to second it and shoulder it forward till it stands there in a kind of serene astronomic solitude and remoteness, — is a vision that always shakes the heart of the beholder.

Later in the day we continued our course up the bay through much drift ice, and were soon in sight of two large glaciers, the Turner and the Hubbard. Both presented long, high palisades of ice to the water, like the Muir, but were far less active and explosive. The Hubbard Glacier is just at the sharp bend of the elbow, a regular "fiddler's" elbow, where the bay, much narrowed, turns abruptly from northeast to south. Here, with a Yakutat Indian for pilot, we entered upon the strange and weird scenery of Russell Fiord, and into waters that no ship as large as ours had before navigated. This part of the bay is in size like the Hudson and about sixty miles in length, but how wild and savage! A succession of mountains of almost naked rock, now scored and scalloped and polished by the old glaciers, now with vast moraines upon their sides or heaped at their feet, which the rains and melting snows have plowed and ribbed and carved into many fantastic forms. There was an air of seclusion and remoteness about it all, as if this had been a special playground of the early ice gods, a nook or alley set apart for them in which to indulge every whim and fancy. And what could be more whimsical or fantastic than yonder glacier playing the mountain goat, clinging to the steep sides of the mountain or breaking over its cliffs and yet falling not, hanging there like a congealed torrent, a silent and motionless shadow. The eye seems baffled. Surely the ice is plunging or will plunge the next second: but no, there it is fixed; it bends over the brink, it foams below, but no sound is heard and no movement is apparent. You see the corrugated surface where it emerges from its great snow reservoir on the mountain summit; it shows deep crevasses where it sweeps down a steep incline, then curves across a terrace, then leaps in solid, fixed foam down the face of the cliff, to which it seems bound as by some magic.

These precipice glaciers apparently move no faster than those in the valley. It is in all cases a subtle, invisible movement, like that of the astronomic bodies. It would seem as if gravity had little to do with it. They do not gain momentum like an avalanche of snow or earth, but creep so slowly that to the lookers-on they are as motionless as the rocks themselves. The grade, the obstacles in the way,

seem to make no difference. One would think that
if a mass of ice, weighing many thousand tons,
hanging upon the face of a mountain-wall steeper
than a house roof, detached itself from the rest at all
and began to move, it would gain momentum and
presently shoot down, as the loosened ice and snow
do from our slate roofs. But it does not. If the temperature of the rocks were suddenly raised as in the
case of the roof, no doubt the glacier would shoot,
but it is not. The under surface of the ice is probably perpetually congealed and perpetually loosened, and the crystallization is constantly broken
and constantly reformed, so that the glacier's motion
is more a creeping than a sliding. The carving and
sculpturing of the rocks is of course done by the
pebbles and boulders beneath the ice, and these
must slide or roll.

We followed the bay or inlet to its head, and
anchored for the night in the large oval that marks
its termination. We were about fifteen miles from
the Pacific, being separated from it by a low, level
moraine of the old glaciers. We were now surrounded by low wooded shores, from which in the
long twilight came the sweet vespers of the little
hermit thrush.

On the 20th another hunting party went out
from the ship, and with an Indian guide climbed
and threaded the snow-covered mountains nearly
all day in quest of bears, but came back as empty

handed as it had set out. The ship in the mean time steamed back ten miles to a side arm of the bay, at the head of which is Hidden Glacier, so called because hidden from view behind a shoulder of the mountain. A broad gravel-bed with a stream winding through it, which the retreating glacier had uncovered, was alone visible from the ship. While Gannett and Gilbert proceeded to survey and map the glacier, many of us wandered on shore amid a world of moraines and gravel-banks. In the afternoon we moved to the vicinity of the Hubbard Glacier, where the ship took a fresh supply of water from a mountain torrent, while the glacier hunters viewed the Nunatak Glacier, and the mineralogists with their hammers prowled upon the shore. My own diversion that afternoon was to climb one of the near mountains to an altitude of about twenty-five hundred feet, where I looked down at a fearful angle into the sea, and where I found my first titlark's nest. The bird with her shining eyes looked out upon me, and upon the sublime scene, from a little cavity in a mossy bank near the snow-line. Her nest held six dark-brown eggs. Some pussy willows near by were just starting. I thought to reach the peak of the mountain up a broad and very steep band of snow, but I looked back once too often. The descent to the sea was too easy and too fearful for my imagination, so I cautiously turned back. In a large patch of alders at the foot of the mountain four or five species of birds were nesting and in song. The most welcome sight to me was a solitary barn swallow skimming along as one might have seen it at home, — no barns within hundreds of miles, yet the little swallow seemed quite at her ease.

While we were anchored here, we had another brief vision of surpassing mountain grandeur. The fair weather divinities brushed aside the veil of clouds, and one of the lofty peaks to the north, probably Vancouver, stood revealed to us. We yielded to its mighty spell for a few moments, and then the cloud curtain again dropped.

The next day we left Russell Fiord, and anchored before an Indian encampment below Haenke Island, on the south side of the head of Yakutat Bay. The Indians had come up from their village below, — some of them, we were told, from as far away as Sitka. They were living here in tents and bark huts, and hunting the hair seal amid the drifting icebergs that the Turner and the Hubbard cast off. This was their summer camp; they were laying in a supply of skins and oil against their winter needs. In July they go to the salmon streams and secure their stores of salmon. During these excursions their village at Yakutat is nearly deserted. The encampment we visited was upon the beach of a broad, gravelly delta flanked by high mountains. It was redolent of seal oil. The dead carcasses of the seals lay in rows upon the pebbles in front of the tents and huts. The women and girls were skinning them, and cutting out the blubber and trying it out in pots over smouldering fires, while the crack of the men's shotguns could be heard out amid the ice. Apparently their only food at such times is seal meat, with parts of the leaf or stalk of a kind of cow-parsnip, a coarse, rank plant that grows all about. The Indian women frowned upon our photographers, and were very averse to having the cameras pointed at them. It took a good deal of watching and waiting and manœuvring to get a good shot. The artists, with their brushes and canvases, were regarded with less suspicion.

The state of vegetation in Yakutat Bay was like that of early May in New York, though the temperature was lower. Far up the mountain-side near the line of snow the willows were just pushing out. At their base the columbine, rock-loving as at home, but larger and coarser-flowered, was in bloom, and blue violets could be gathered by the handful. Back of the encampment were acres of lupine just bursting into flower. It gave a gay, festive look to the place. Red-vested bumble-bees were working eagerly upon it. The yellow warbler was nesting in the alders near by. New birds added to our list from these shores were the pine grosbeak, the Arctic tern, and the robber jaeger. No large game was secured by our hunters in Yakutat Bay, though Captain Kelly declared he was at one time so near a bear

Alaska Indians

that he could smell him. The bear undoubtedly got a smell of the captain first.

Our party had now been a month together, and had assumed the features of a large and happy family on a summer holiday cruise. We were of diverse interests and types of character, yet one in the spirit of true comradeship. This fortunate condition was due largely to the truly democratic and manly character of the head of the expedition, Mr. Harriman, and to the cheerful and obliging temper of Captain Doran. The pleasure of the party was the pleasure of our host and of the captain. The ship was equally at the service of men who wanted to catch mice or collect a new bird, and of those who wanted to survey a glacier or inlet or to shoot a bear. One day it made a voyage of sixty miles to enable our collectors to take up some traps, the total catch of which proved to be nine mice. The next day it was as likely to go as far to enable Ritter and Saunders to dredge for new forms of sea life, or Devereux to inspect some outcropping of copper ore. Early in the voyage our committee on entertainment arranged a course of lectures. Nearly every night at eight o'clock, on the upper deck or in the Social Hall, some one of our college professors or government specialists held forth. One night it was Dall upon the history or geography of Alaska; then Gilbert upon the agency of glaciers in shaping the valleys and mountains, or upon the glaciers we had recently visited; then Brewer upon climate and ocean currents, or Coville upon some botanical features of the regions about us, or Ritter upon the shore forms of sea life, or Emerson upon volcanoes and lava beds, or John Muir on his experiences upon the glaciers and his adventure with his dog Stikeen in crossing a huge crevasse on a sliver of ice, or Charles Keeler on the coloration of birds, or Fuertes on bird-songs, or Grinnell on Indian tribes and Indian characteristics, and so on. On Sunday evenings Dr. Nelson conducted the Episcopal service and preached a sermon, while at other times books and music and games added to the attraction of the Social Hall.

PRINCE WILLIAM SOUND

After several days in Yakutat Bay we steamed northward again, bound for Prince William Sound. The fog and cloud hid the St. Elias Range, but the great Malaspina Glacier was visible on our right. This is the largest of the Alaskan glaciers, covering fifteen hundred square miles. It has a front of fifty miles on the sea, and runs back thirty miles to the St. Elias Range, from which it is fed. It is a vast plain of ice, with lakes and rivers, and with hills of rocks and gravel that have trees and alders growing upon them. One of our hunting parties touched the skirts of it, and saw where the earth and alders had slid off over quite an area, exposing the ice. Its

Yakutat side seems stagnant; it no longer discharges bergs into the sea, and will in time probably
drop its vast burden of medial moraine upon the
ground beneath. We caught glimpses of its numerous feeders below the clouds along the base
of St. Elias, but of the glacier itself we saw only the
earth-covered margin it presents to the sea. The
discharge of roily water from beneath it is so great
that it colors the sea over an area equal to its own;
"glacier milk," some one called it, and it gives the
Pacific a milky tinge for thirty miles offshore.

I must not forget the albatross that found us out
and followed our ship when we had been but a few
hours at sea, wheeling around us close to the water,
coming and going, now on one side, now on the
other, slanting and curving, and all on straight,
unbending wing. Its apparently toilless, effortless
flight and its air of absolute leisure were very curious and striking, — it seemed like the spirit of the
deep taking visible form and seeking to weave some
spell upon us or lure us away to destruction. Never
before had I seen flying so easy and spontaneous, —
not an action, not a thought, not an effort, but a
dream. What a contrast to the flight of the Arctic
tern which we first saw in Yakutat Bay, a bird with
long, sickle-shaped wings, with which it fairly reaped
the air. The flight of the albatross was a series of
long, graceful strokes, unlike that of any other bird
I have ever seen.

About noon on the 24th, amid fog and light rain, we sighted Middleton Island on our starboard, when the ship turned her head sharply northward toward the entrance to the sound. In a few hours we ran out of the fog into clear skies, and were soon steaming across the great sound in warm sunshine. Our route was a devious one: past islands and headlands, then over the immense expanse of the open water with a circle of towering, snow-capped mountains far off along the horizon, then winding through arms and straits, close to tree-tufted islands and steep, spruce-clad mountains, now looking between near-by dark forested hills upon a group of distant peaks white as midwinter, then upon broad, low, wooded shores with glimpses of open, meadow-like glades among the trees, suggesting tender grass and grazing herds, till in the early evening we sighted a little cluster of buildings peeping out of the forest at the base of a lofty mountain. This was Orca, where there is a large salmon cannery and a post-office. Here we anchored for the night. In the long twilight some of our party climbed to the top of the mountain, twenty-five hundred feet in height, and brought back a native heather, — bryanthus, — in bloom. Others of us wandered upon the beach, and engaged in conversation with some gold-seekers just out from Copper River. They were encamped here, waiting for a steamer to take them away and for funds from friends at home to enable

68

them to get away. It was a story of hardships and disappointment that they had to tell us, — yes, and of scurvy and death. Over three thousand men had gone into the Copper River region a year or more before on the wildest, vaguest rumor of gold. They had gone in hurriedly and slyly, as it were, so as to be ahead of the crowd. Each man had taken supplies to last him a year, at least. Now they were coming out destitute and without one cent's worth of gold; many of them had died. Scurvy had broken out among them, had swept away scores of them, and had lamed and disabled others. Their toils and privations had been terrible; snow, glaciers, mountains, swollen rivers, had blocked their way. Most of them had abandoned their unconsumed supplies and extra blankets, content to get out with their lives. They were from the East and from the West, lumbermen from Maine and Pennsylvania and old miners from California and Colorado. They were a sturdy, sober-looking set of men that we saw, no nonsense about them. Such hardships and disappointments seem to sweep away everything affected and meretricious in a man, and uncover and bring out the bedrock of character, if there is any in him. In this crowd two large, powerful men, father and son, were especially noticeable. The father, a man probably of sixty-five years, had nearly died with scurvy and was still very lame, and the tenderness and solicitude of the son toward him warmed my heart, — homely, slow, deliberate men, but evidently made of the real stuff. These stranded men were penniless, and were depending upon the charity, or the willingness to trust, of the steamboat company to take them home to San Francisco. I was glad when I saw them depart on the steamer the next day. Alaska is full of such adventurers ransacking the land. We heard of them at several other points: men looking for new Klondikes, exploring remote corners, going eagerly and quietly into the wilderness, crossing glaciers, rivers, and mountains, hoping to be the first in new and rich fields.

Sunday the 25th was another day of great beauty. We spent the main part of it steaming across the sound toward some of the more remote inlets. It was an ideal day, an ideal sail; a day to bask in the sunshine upon the upper deck and leisurely contemplate the vast shifting panorama of sea and islands and wooded shores and towering peaks spread before us on every hand; a day that gave us another feast of beauty and sublimity, and that stands out in the memory unforgettable! We were afloat in an enchanted circle; we sailed over magic seas under magic skies; we played hide and seek with winter in lucid sunshine over blue and emerald waters, — all the conditions, around, above, below us were most fortunate.

Prince William Sound is shaped like a great spider: an open, irregular body of water eighty miles

or more across, fringed with numerous arms and
inlets that reach far in amid the mountains. Across
the head of most of these arms are huge glaciers;
others hang upon the mountain-sides or cascade
down them. It was toward the head of one of these
inlets that we were now bound. In the afternoon we
reached its end, and saw another palisade of shattered ice, about two hundred feet high and four
miles long, barring our way. We named this the
Columbia Glacier. Its front was quite as imposing
as that of the Muir, but it was less active; apparently no large blue bergs are born out of its depth,
for the reason, doubtless, that its depth is not great.
On a wooded island near its front we left two of our
geologists to survey and report upon it. At eight
o'clock that Sunday evening we were at anchor in
Virgin Bay, with low, partly wooded islands on the
one hand, and sloping open shores at the foot of tall
mountains on the other. Two or three small houses
were seen scattered along the shore on the margin of
these broad, natural, grassy clearings. Copper ore
had been found here and there near the cabins of the
prospectors. On two of the islands near us were fox
farms. One of the farmers came off in his boat to
see us, and talked intelligently about his enterprise.
His foxes would swim to an adjoining island a few
hundred yards away, so his brother had established
a fox farm there. Blue foxes are the species cul-
tivated ; their main food in winter is dried fish

caught during the summer out of the surrounding waters. Each island contained several hundred acres, mostly covered with spruce. Upon the subject of profits he could not yet speak, as the enterprise was new. We here saw our first Eskimo. He came paddling toward our ship in a double kyak, and as our naphtha launch circled about him, he had an amused, childish look.

We put a party ashore to spend a couple of days hunting and collecting. After the Sunday evening service, the sun was still glowing upon the distant white peaks, and a dozen or more of us seized the occasion to go ashore and walk in the long twilight upon the strange land. How novel and bewitching it all was! The open meadow-like expanse near the beach proved to be tundra, — wet, spongy, mossy, grassy, and full of wild flowers, the most conspicuously beautiful of which was the shooting-star or dodecatheon. Our collectors had pitched their tents near the log cabin of two prospectors, on a point of land at the mouth of a clear, rapid stream. The hermit thrush sang in the forest close by ; the stream sang, and the air under the shadow of the mountain was pervaded with a strange peace and charm. The only singing that was not so agreeable was that of the mosquitoes, but amid such scenes petty annoyances are soon forgotten. One of the prospectors, a brisk little man, whose clean, snug cabin we visited, was born near North Cape in Norway. He had been here over a year, and as our ladies were the first who had ever visited his camp, he took off his hat and, with his hand upon his heart, made a gallant bow to them in acknowledgment. He was planning to go to the Paris Exposition next year, and life seemed to offer him many bright outlooks.

The next day, Monday the 26th, we spent in Port Wells, the extreme northeast arm of the sound, taking in water from a foaming mountain torrent and again coquetting with glaciers. The weather was fair, but the sea air was cold. Indeed, we were in another great ice chest, — glaciers to right of us, glaciers to left of us, glaciers in front of us, volleyed and thundered; the mountains were ribbed with them, and the head of the bay was walled with them. At one time we could see five, separated by intervals of a few miles, cascading down from the heights, while the chief of the flock was booming incessantly at the head of the valley. The two large glaciers at the head of the fiord were named by our party Harvard and Yale; the cascading glaciers on the west side, Radcliffe, Smith, Bryn Mawr, Vassar, and Wellesley; and the main glacier on the east side of Port Wells, Amherst. On going ashore we had a chance to view, in profile, those pouring down from the heights, and the effect was novel and strange. We looked along the green, tender enfoliaged side of the mountain and saw one of these torrents of shattered ice rising up fifty or more feet above its banks,

73

and as if about to topple over upon them; but it did not. To the eye it was as fixed as the rocks; apparently one could have leaned his back against the ice with his feet upon the foliage. The channel of Port Wells was so blocked with ice from the incessant discharges of the glaciers that the ship made her way with great difficulty, and was finally compelled to anchor more than twenty miles from the head. In the launches we managed to get about ten miles nearer. This was the most active glacier we had seen. The thundering of the great ice Niagara there in the distance was in our ears every moment, but we could not get near it; it beat us off with its ice avalanches. Such piles of gravel and broken rocks as I climbed and tried to cross that day at the foot of one of the lesser side glaciers dwarfed anything I had yet seen. They suggested the crush of mountains and the wreck of continents.

Two things constantly baffle and mislead the eye in all these Alaskan waters — size and distance. Things are on a new scale. The standard one brings with him will not hold. The eye says it is three miles to such a point, it turns out to be six; or that the front of yonder glacier is a hundred feet high, and it is two hundred or more. For my part, I never succeeded in bringing my eye up to the Alaskan scale. Many a point, many a height, which I marked for my own from the deck of the ship, seemed to recede from me when I turned my steps toward it. The wonderfully clear air probably had something to do with the illusion. Forms were so distinct that one fancied them near at hand when they were not.

On shore we found gulls and Arctic terns nesting on little sandy hillocks, and saw oyster-catchers, a ptarmigan, and the wandering tattler. In the water the marbled murrelets were common ; with their short wings and plump, round bodies they looked like sea quail. Our first and only mishap to the ship in these waters befell us here, — the breaking of one of the blades of the propeller upon a cake of ice, an accident that had the effect of making our craft limp a little.

HARRIMAN FIORD

Later in the afternoon we ascended an arm of Port Wells more to the westward and entered upon a voyage of discovery. We steamed up to a glacier of prodigious size that reared its front across the head of the inlet and barred further progress in that direction, — the Barry Glacier. According to the U. S. Coast Survey map we were at the end of navigation in these waters, but Mr. Harriman suggested to the captain that he take the ship a little nearer the glacier, when a way seemed open to the left. As we progressed, the mountains fell apart and a passage opened there around the corner, like a street coming in at right angles to a main thoroughfare.

The captain naturally hesitated to enter it; it was unmapped and unsounded water.

"Go ahead, Captain," said Mr. Harriman, "I will take the risk."

We went on under a good head of steam up this new inlet, where no ship had ever before passed. It was one of the most exciting moments of our voyage. We could see another huge glacier about ten miles ahead of us, with its front on the water barring the way. Glaciers hung on the steep mountain-sides all about us. Some of them, as Mr. Elliot said, looked like the stretched skins of huge polar bears. The scene was wild and rugged in the extreme. One of the glaciers was self-named the Serpentine by reason of its winding course down from its hidden sources in the mountains, — a great white serpent with its jaws set with glittering fangs at the sea. Another was self-named the Stairway, as it came down in regular terraces or benches. A Colossus of Rhodes with seven-league boots would have been an appropriate figure upon it. As we neared the front of this last glacier, the mountains to the left again parted and opened up another new arm of the sea, with more glaciers tumbling in mute sublimity from the heights, or rearing colossal palisades across our front. A ten-mile course brought us to the head of this inlet, which was indeed the end of navigation in this direction. Here we left Gannett and Muir to survey and bring to map our new bit of geography. Subsequently this inlet was fitly named Harriman Fiord, and the glacier at the head of it, Harriman Glacier.

In no very distant past, the various ice sheets, united in one body, had filled the inlet to the mountain's brim — a vast ice monster. Now, the body of the monster is gone and his limbs lie upon the mountains on either side, while his tail and rump are at the head of the main valley.

Our vessel, on coming out of the inlet and turning almost at right angles into Port Wells, was caught by the very strong ebb tide, which for a moment held her in its grasp. She hesitated to respond to her helm, and was making direct for the face of the great glacier on our port side; but presently she came about, as if aware of her danger, and went on her way in less agitated waters.

This great glacier, — the Barry, — which guards the entrance to Harriman Inlet, presented some novel features; among others, huge archways above the water-line, suggesting entrances to some walled city. When masses of ice fell, I fancied I could hear the reverberation in these arched caverns.

The next day, which was thick and rainy, we picked up our party at Virgin Bay, and steamed back to Orca to mend our broken propeller. I wondered how it could be done, as there is no dry dock there, but the problem proved an easy one. The tide is so great in these waters that every shelving beach

becomes a dry dock at low tide. In the morning our
steamer lay in shallow water on the beach at Orca.
A low scaffolding was built around her propeller,
and very soon the broken blade was replaced by a
new one. While this was being done, many of us
viewed the process of salmon canning. Some of the
fish lay piled up on the dock, and were being loaded
into wheelbarrows with a one-tined pitchfork and
wheeled in to the cleaners. Most of the work was
done by Chinamen from San Francisco. It was positively fascinating to see the skill and swiftness with
which some of these men worked ; only two used
knives, — long, thin blades, which they kept very
sharp. They cut off the fins, severed the head and
tail, and did the disemboweling with lightning-like
rapidity. It was like the tricks of jugglers. There
was a gleam of steel about the fish half a moment
and the work was done. One had to be very intent
to follow the movements. The fish were then washed
and scraped and passed on to workmen inside,
where they were cut and packed by machinery.
Every second all day long a pound can, snugly
packed, drops from the ingenious mechanism. For
some reason the looker-on soon loses his taste for
salmon, there is such a world of it. It is as common as chips; it is kicked about under foot; it lies
in great sweltering heaps; many of the fish, while
lying upon the beach before they are brought in, are
pecked and bruised by gulls and ravens ; the air is

redolent of an odor far different from that of roses or new-mown hay, and very shortly one turns away to the woods or to the unpolluted beach.

The first tide was not high enough to lift our steamer, so we passed another day at Orca, and all hands went in the naphtha launches on a picnic to a wild place eight or ten miles distant with the suggestive name of Bomb Point. It was a lovely secluded spot, a crescent-shaped beach half a mile long at the head of a shallow bay, flanked by low, wooded points and looked down upon by lofty mountains. Here we were quickly roaming over one of those large natural clearings or hyperborean meadows that we had so often seen from the ship, and that had looked so friendly and enticing. This one, on a nearer view, proved especially alluring and delightful ; a strange air of privacy and seclusion was over it all. It was not merely carpeted to the foot, it was cushioned. Walking over it was like walking over a feather-bed, — moss and grass a foot deep or more upon a foundation of soft peat. Wild flowers — yellow, white, pink, purple — were everywhere.

Little pools or basins of brown water, their brims neatly faced and rounded with moss and grass, were sunk here and there into the surface. Stunted mossy hemlocks and spruces dotted the landscape, and the near-by woods threw out irregular lines of gray, moss-draped trees, — novel, interesting. Such a look of age, and yet the bloom and dimples of youth!

Bearded, decrepit, dwarfed spruces above a turf like a pillow decked with flowers! I walked along a margin of open woods that had a singularly genial, sheltered, home look, and listened to the hermit thrush. The nearer we get to the region of perpetual snow, the more does vegetable life seem to simulate snow and cover the ground with softness, — softness to the foot, and dimpled surface to the eye. Such handfuls of wild flowers as we all gathered! The thought in every one's mind was, Oh, if we could only place these flowers in the hands of friends at home! The colors were all deep and intense.

In the afternoon the steamer picked us up. A little after midnight we took aboard the party we had left at Columbia Glacier, and then returned to Harriman Fiord for Gannett and Muir. When they were on board, we once more turned our faces to the open sea, bound for Cook Inlet, the largest of the Alaskan bays. It penetrates the land one hundred and fifty miles, and is more than fifty miles broad at its mouth.

We entered it on the 30th, under bright skies, and dropped anchor behind a low sandspit in Kachemac Bay, on the end of which is a group of four or five buildings making up the hamlet of Homer. There was nothing Homeric in the look of the place, but grandeur looked down upon it from the mountains around, especially from the great volcanic peaks, Iliamna and Redoubt, sixty miles across the inlet to the west. The former rises over twelve thousand feet from the sea and, bathed in sunshine, was an impressive spectacle. It was wrapped in a mantle of snow, but it evidently was warm at heart, for we could see steam issuing from two points near its summit.

Our stay in Cook Inlet was brief. Our hunters had hoped to kill some big game here, but after interviewing an experienced hunter who had a camp on shore, they concluded that on our return in July the prospects would be better. On the afternoon of June 30, therefore, we left the inlet and were off for the island of Kadiak, a hundred miles to the southwest.

KADIAK

We were now about to turn over a new leaf, or indeed to open a new book, and to enter upon an entirely different type of scenery, — the treeless type. Up to this point, or for nearly two thousand miles, we had seen the mountains and valleys covered with unbroken spruce forests. Now we were to have two thousand miles without a tree, the valleys and mountains green as a lawn, and to the eye as smooth, — all of volcanic origin; many of the cones ideally perfect; the valleys deepened and carved by the old glaciers, and heights and lowlands alike covered with a carpet of grass, ferns, and flowers.

The forests begin to fail at the mouth of Cook Inlet. As we came out, my eye was drawn to rolling heights, where were groups and lines of trees amid broad, green expanses. The suggestion of hill farms at home with orchards and groves, and trees along the fences, was very strong, but one looked in vain for the houses and barns of the farmers. We were going into a milder climate, too. During nearly all the month of June, despite my extra winter clothing, I had suffered with cold. In Prince William Sound and in Yakutat Bay we were in vast refrigerating chests. The air had all been on ice, and the sunshine seemed only to make us feel its tooth the more keenly. With benumbed fingers I wrote to a friend in this strain: "Amid your summer weather, do remember us in our wanderings, a-chill on these northern seas, beleaguered by icebergs, frowned upon by glaciers, and held as by some enchantment in a vast circle of snow-capped mountain peaks. Are your hands and feet really warm? Is it true that there is no snow upon the mountains?"

But balmier skies awaited us; the warmer currents of the Pacific flowing up from Japan and the southern seas were soon to breathe upon us; that pastoral paradise, Kadiak, was soon to greet us.

All the afternoon we steamed along the coast in smooth seas, in full view of lofty, snow-covered mountains with huge glaciers issuing from out their loins. Late at night, off against Kukak Bay, we put off a party of five or six men who wished to spend a week collecting and botanizing on the mainland. It looked like a perilous piece of business, the debarkation of these men in the darkness, in an open boat on an unknown coast many miles from shore. Might they not miss the bay? Might they not find the surf running too high to land, or might not some other mishap befall them? But after a hard pull of several hours, they made the shore at a suitable landing-place, and their days spent there were in every way satisfactory.

On the morning of July 1, we woke up in Uyak Bay on the north side of the Island of Kadiak. The sky was clear and the prospect most inviting. Smooth, treeless, green hills and mountains surrounded us, pleasing to the eye and alluring to the feet. Two large salmon canneries were visible on shore, and presently a boat came off to us with fresh salmon. Here we left a naphtha launch with a party of six men, heavily armed, bent on finding and killing the great Kadiak bear, the largest species of bear in the world, as big as an ox. They had been making up their mouths for this monster bear all the way, and now they were at last close to his haunts. In two or three days we were to return and pick them up and hoist their game aboard with the great derrick. In the delicious sunshine we steamed out of Uyak, bound for Kadiak village on the east end of the island, one hundred miles away. Kadiak Island lies nearly south from Cook Inlet, about fifty miles from the mainland. It is one hundred and fifty miles long and one third as broad. It would just about fill up Cook Inlet, out of which it may have slipped some time for aught I know. It is treeless except upon the east end, which faces toward the great Alaskan forests, from which the tree infection may have come.

How beautiful and interesting the shores we passed that day ! Smooth, rounded hills, as green and tender to the eye as well-kept lawns, recalling the hills we saw in May upon Snake River ; natural sheep ranges, such as one sees in the north of England, but not a sign of life upon them.

I warn my reader here, that henceforth I shall babble continually of green fields. There was no end to them. We had come from an arboreal wilderness to a grassy wilderness, from a world of spruce forests to a world of emerald heights and verdant slopes. Look at the map of Alaska, and think of all the peninsulas from Cook Inlet and all the adjacent islands, and the long chain of the Aleutians sweeping nearly across to Asia, as being covered with an unbroken carpet of verdure, — it must needs be the main feature in my descriptions. Never had I seen such beauty of greenness, because never before had I seen it from such a vantage-ground of blue sea.

We had not been many hours out of Uyak that afternoon when we began to see a few scattered spruce-trees, then patches of forest in the valley bottoms. At one point we passed near a large natural park. It looked as if a landscape gardener might have been employed to grade and shape the ground, and

plant it with grass and trees in just the right propor-
tion. Here were cattle, too, and how good they looked,
grazing or reposing on those long, smooth vistas between the trees! To eyes sated with the wild, austere grandeur of Prince William Sound the change
was most delightful. Our course lay through narrow
channels and over open bays sprinkled with green
islands, past bold cliffs and headlands, till at three
o'clock we entered the narrow strait, no more than
twice the ship's length in width, upon which is situated the village of Kadiak, called by the Russians
St. Paul. We could see the wild flowers upon the
shore as we passed along, barn swallows twittered
by, a magpie crossed the strait from one green bank
to the other, and as we touched the wharf a song
sparrow was singing from the weather-vane of a
large warehouse, — a song sparrow in voice, man-
ners, and color, but in form twice as large as our
home bird. The type of song sparrow changes all
the way from Yakutat Bay to the Aleutian Islands,
till at the latter place it is nearly as large as the catbird; but the song and general habits of the bird
change but very little. How welcome the warmth,
too! We had stepped from April into June, with the
mercury near the seventies, and our spirits rose
accordingly. How we swarmed out of the ship, like
boys out of school, longing for a taste of grass and of
the rural seclusion and sweetness! That great green
orb or half orb of a mountain that shone down upon

us from just back of the town, the highest point in
its rim at an altitude of twenty-three hundred feet,
— how our legs tingled to climb it! and the green
vale below, where the birds were singing and many
rare wild flowers blooming; and the broad, gentle
height to the north, threaded by a grassy lane, where
groves of low, fragrant spruces promised a taste
of the blended sylvan and pastoral; or the smooth,
rounded island opposite, over which the sea threw
blue glances; or the curving line of water sweeping
away to the south toward a rugged mountain-
wall, streaked with snow; or the peaceful, quaint
old village itself, strung upon paths and grassy lanes,
with its chickens and geese and children, and two or
three cows cropping the grass or ruminating by the
wayside, — surely, here was a tempting field to ship-
bound voyagers from the chilly and savage north.
The town itself had a population of seven or eight
hundred people, Indians, half-breeds, and Russians,
with a sprinkling of Americans, living in comfortable frame cottages, generally with a bit of garden
attached. The people fish, hunt the sea-otter, and
work for the Alaska Commercial Company. We
met here an old Vermonter, a refined, scholarly
looking man, with a patriarchal beard, who had
married a native woman and had a family of young
children growing up around him. He liked the climate better than that of New England. The winters
were not very cold, never below zero, and the sum-

mers were not hot, rarely up to 80° Fahrenheit.
There were no horses or wheeled vehicles in town,
and the streets were grassy lanes. Such a rural,
Arcadian air I had never before seen pervading a
town upon American soil. There is a Greek church
near the wharf, and its chime of bells was in our
ears for hours at a time. The only incongruous
thing I saw was a building with a big sign on its
ridge-board: "Chicago Store." I went in and asked
for some fresh eggs; they had none, but directed
me to a cottage near the beach.

I found here a large Russian woman, who had the
eggs, for which, after consulting with a younger
woman, she wanted "four bits." The potatoes in
her garden had tops a foot high, but her currant-
bushes were just in bloom. Our stay of five days in
this charming place was a dream of rural beauty and
repose: warm summer skies above us, green, flower-
strewn hills and slopes around us, — our paths were
indeed in green pastures and beside still waters.
One enticing trail left the old Russian road half a
mile north of the village, and led off northwest across
little mossy and flowery glens, through spruce
groves, over little runs, up a shoulder of the mountain, and then down a few miles into a broad,
green, silent valley that held a fine trout brook.
The path was probably made by the village anglers.
In looking into such a peaceful, verdant sweep of
country, one almost instinctively looked for farm-

houses, or for flocks and herds and other signs of human occupancy; but they were not there. One high mountain that cut into the valley at right angles had a long, easy ridge, apparently as sharp as the ridge-board of a building. I marked it for my own and thought to set my feet upon it, but the way was too beguiling, and I did not get there. The mountain looked as though it had just had a priming-coat of delicate green paint.

But the mighty emerald billow that rose from the rear of the village, — we all climbed that, some of us repeatedly. From the ship it looked as smooth as a meadow, but the climber soon found himself knee deep in ferns, grasses, and a score of flowering plants, and now and then was forced to push through a patch of alders as high as his head. He could not go far before his hands would be full of flowers, blue predominating. The wild geranium here is light blue, and tinges the slopes as daisies and buttercups do at home. Near the summit were patches of a most exquisite forget-me-not of a pure, delicate blue with yellow centre. It grew to the height of a foot, and a handful of it looked like something just caught out of the sky above. Here, too, was a small, delicate lady's-slipper, pale yellow striped with maroon ; also a dwarf rhododendron, its large purple flowers sitting upon the moss and lichen. The climber also waded through patches of lupine, and put his feet upon bluebells, Jacob's ladder, iris, saxifrage,

cassiope, and many others. The song-birds that
attracted our notice were the golden-crowned sparrow and the little hermit thrush. The golden-crown
has a strangely piercing, plaintive song, very simple,
but very appealing. It consists of only three notes,
but they come from out the depths of the bird's soul.
In them is all the burden of the mystery and the
pathos of life.

In the spruce groves to the north opened up by
the old grassy road, besides the birds named, one
heard the pine grosbeak, the gray-cheeked thrush,
and the weird strain of the Oregon robin. This last
bird was very shy and hard to get a view of. I reclined
for two hours one day upon the deep dry moss under
the spruces, waiting for the singer to reveal himself.
When seen he looks like our robin in a holiday suit.
His song is a long, tapering note or whistle, at times
with a peculiar tolling effect.

TO THE OREGON ROBIN IN ALASKA

O Varied Thrush! O Robin strange!
  Behold my mute surprise.
Thy form and flight I long have known,
  But not this new disguise.

I do not know thy slaty coat,
  Nor vest with darker zone ;
I 'm puzzled by thy recluse ways
  And song in monotone.

FAR AND NEAR

I left thee 'mid my orchard's bloom,
    When May had crowned the year ;
Thy nest was on the apple bough,
    Where rose thy carol clear.

Thou lurest now through fragrant shades,
    Where hoary spruces grow ;
Where floor of moss infolds the foot,
    Like depths of fallen snow.

Loquacious ravens clack and croak
    Nor hold me in my quest ;
The purple grosbeaks perch and sing
    Upon the cedar's crest.

But thou art doomed to shun the day,
    A captive of the shade ;
I only catch thy stealthy flight
    Athwart the forest glade.

Thy voice is like a hermit's reed
    That solitude beguiles ;
Again 't is like a silver bell
    Adrift in forest aisles.

Throw off, throw off this masquerade
    And don thy ruddy vest,
And let me find thee, as of old,
    Beside thy orchard nest.

While here Mr. Harriman had the luck to kill the long-expected Kadiak bear; he shot a mother and cub. He and his guide, an old Russian named Stepan Kondakoff, found her grazing near the snow-line on the mountain-side about ten miles to the south. She was eating grass like a cow, Mr. Harriman said. She was a large animal, but below the size of the traditional Kadiak bear. Her color was a faded brown. A much larger one was seen far across a difficult valley.

On July 3, which was bright and warm, a number of us visited Wood Island, a few miles to the east, where the North American Commercial Company has its headquarters, and where are large old spruce woods and lakes of fresh water. Charles Keeler and I heard, or fancied we heard, voices calling us from out the depths of the woods; so we left the party and took ourselves thither, and lounged for hours in the mossy, fragrant solitudes, eating our lunch by a little rill of cold water, listening to the song-birds and ravens, and noting the wood flowers and moss-draped trees. Here we heard the winter wren at our leisure, a bubbling, trilling, prolonged strain like that of our eastern bird, but falling far short of it in melody and in wild lyrical penetration. In other words, it was the same song sung by a far inferior voice. The elusive note of the Oregon robin, as though the dark, motionless spruces had found a voice, was also heard here and there. These woods were not merely carpeted with moss, they were upholstered ; the ground was padded ankle-deep, and under every tree was a couch of the most luxurious kind.

The 4th of July found us, as it usually finds Americans, wherever they are, overflowing with patriotism, bunting, and gunpowder hilarity. Our huge graphophone played very well the part of a brass band; Professor Brewer, upon the hurricane deck, discharged admirably the duties of the orator of the day; he was followed by Mr. Keeler, who shaded the picture the speaker had drawn by a stirring poem, touching upon some of the nation's shortcomings ; songs and music, followed by a boat race and general merriment, finished the programme.

Kadiak, I think, won a place in the hearts of all of us. Our spirits probably touched the highest point here. If we had other days that were epic, these days were lyric. To me they were certainly more exquisite and thrilling than any before or after. I feel as if I wanted to go back to Kadiak, almost as if I could return there to live, — so secluded, so remote, so peaceful; such a mingling of the domestic, the pastoral, the sylvan, with the wild and the rugged; such emerald heights, such flowery vales, such blue arms and recesses of the sea, and such a vast green solitude stretching away to the west and to the north and to the south. Bewitching Kadiak! the spell of thy summer freshness and placidity is still upon me.

On the 5th, still under clear, warm skies, we left this

92

rural paradise and steamed away to Kukak Bay on the mainland, to pick up the party we had left there on the night of June 30. It was a relief to find they had had no misadventure and were well pleased with their expedition. They described one view that made the listener wish he had been with them: they had climbed to the top of a long green slope behind their camp, and had suddenly found themselves on the brink of an almost perpendicular mountain-wall. Through a deep notch in this wall they had looked down two thousand feet into a valley beneath them invaded by a great glacier that swept down from the snow-white peaks beyond. The spectacle was so unexpected and so tremendous that it fairly took their breaths away. From the deck of the ship the slope up which their course lay looked like a piece of stretched green baize cloth.

An event of this day's cruising which I must not forget was the strange effects wrought for us by that magician *Mirage :* islands and headlands in the air, long, low capes doubled, one above another, with a lucid space between them ; a level snowy range standing up slightly above a nearer rocky one, drawn out and manipulated till it suggested a vast Grecian temple crowning a rocky escarpment, — fantasy, illusion, enchantment, — trick played with sea and shore on every hand that afternoon.

From this point we turned to the island again, and in the middle of the night gathered in the bear hunters we had left at Uyak Bay. They were bearless, but they had the comfort of having seen many signs of bears, of having had many enjoyable tramps over hill and across dale in a green, treeless country, of having found a superb waterfall, and of having survived the hordes of mosquitoes.

We steamed all day southwestward along the Alaska Peninsula, under clear skies and over smooth waters, past the Semides and on to the Shumagin Islands, where we dropped anchor about midnight.

When we put our heads out of our windows on the morning of the 7th, we were at anchor off Sand Point, in a bay in Popof Island, one of the Shumagin group, about halfway down the Alaska Peninsula. On the one hand we saw a low, green, treeless slope, almost within a stone's throw, from which came many musical bird voices. The lesser hermit thrush, the golden-crowned sparrow, the fox sparrow, the large song sparrow, the yellow warbler, the rosy finch, all were distinguishable from the ship's deck. It is a novel experience to wake up in the morning on an ocean steamer and hear bird-songs through one's open window, but this was often our experience on this trip. On this grassy hill are some curious volcanic warts or excrescences that give a strange effect to the scene. On the other hand, the blue waters of the harbor stretch away to low, alder-clad shores, from which rise a range of bare volcanic mountains, among them one perfect cone, probably three thousand feet high.

In the Shumagins three men elected to leave the ship to dredge the sea and study the volcanic formation of the land. We promised to pick them up on our return ten days hence. At ten o'clock our anchor was up and we were off for Unalaska. The event of this day was the view we had of the twin volcanic peaks of Pavlof, rising from the shore to an altitude of seven or eight thousand feet. One of them was a symmetrical cone, with black converging lines of rock cutting through the snow like the ribs of an umbrella; the other was more rugged and irregular, with many rents upon its sides and near its summit, from which vapors issued, staining the snow like smoke from a chimney. Sheets of vapor were also seen issuing from cracks at its foot near the sea level. We were specially fortunate in viewing these grand mountains under such favorable weather conditions.

On this day also, just after passing Pavlof, we were for hours in sight of the Aghileen Pinnacles, which have such a strange architectural effect amid the wilder and ruder forms that surround them, as if some vast, many-spired cathedral of dark gray stone were going to decay there in the mountain solitude. Both in form and color they seemed alien to everything about them. Now we saw them athwart the crests of smooth green hills, then rising behind

95

naked, rocky ridges, or fretting the sky above lines of snow. Their walls are so steep that no snow lies upon them, while the pinnacles are like church spires.

The whole of the Alaska Peninsula, all the islands off it, the islands in Bering Sea, and the Aleutian group are of volcanic origin, and some of the embers of the old fires are still alive in our day, as we had proof. Since our visit there has been other proof in the shape of a severe earthquake shock felt all along the Alaskan coast, in some places disastrously.

Continuing to the westward, we sailed along verdant shores and mountains without sign of human habitation till we saw a cluster of buildings called Belkofski, — two or three dozen brown roofs grouped around a large white, green-topped building, probably a Greek church. The settlement seemed carefully set down there in the green solitude like a toy village on a shelf. The turf had not been anywhere broken; not a mark or stain upon the treeless landscape. Above it ran a smooth, barren mountain, which swept down in green slopes to a broad emerald plain upon which the hamlet sat. Now a long headland comes down to the water's edge with its green carpet; then again it is cut off sharply by the sea, or cut in twain, showing sheer pyramidal walls two hundred feet high. Then a succession of vast, smooth, emerald slopes running up into high, gray, desolate mountains, pointed, conical, curved; now

96

presenting a mighty bowl, fluted and scalloped and opening on one side through a sweep of valley to the sea, then a creased and wrinkled lawn at an angle of forty-five degrees and miles in extent. The motionless ice sheets we had seen farther north flowing down out of the mountains were here simulated by grassy billows flowing down out of the hills. Green, white, and blue are the three prevailing tints all the way from Cook Inlet to Unalaska ; blue of the sea and sky, green of the shores and lower slopes, and white of the lofty peaks and volcanic cones, — they are mingled and contrasted all the way.

Was it on this day also that my eye dwelt so long and so fondly upon what appeared to be another architectural ruin, abutting on the sea and bathed in the soft light of the late afternoon sun ? Was it some old abbey, or was it some unfinished temple to the gods of the mountain ? Two spires, one at either end, stood up many hundred feet, one slender and tapering to a blunt point, with the suggestion of a recess for a bell, the other heavy and massive, and evidently only a stump of what it had been; the roof vast and sloping, the upper story with its windows rudely outlined, and the lower merged in a mass of gray, uncarved rock.

Before nightfall we passed two more notable volcanic peaks, Isanotski and Shishaldin, both of which penetrate the clouds at an altitude of nearly nine thousand feet. These are on Unimak Island at the end of the peninsula. Our first glimpse was of a black cone ending in a point far above a heavy mass of cloud. It seemed buoyed up there by the clouds. There was nothing visible beneath it to indicate the presence of a mountain. Then the clouds blotted it out; but presently the veil was brushed aside again, and before long we saw both mountains from base to summit and noted the vast concave lines of Shishaldin that sweep down to the sea, and mark the typical volcanic form.

The long, graceful curves, so attractive to the eye, repeat on this far-off island the profile of Fuji-Yama, the sacred peak of Japan. Those of our party who had seen Shishaldin in previous years described it as snow white from base to summit. But when we saw it, the upper part, for several thousand feet, was dark, — doubtless the result of heat, for it is smoking this year.

On the morning of the 8th we were tied up at the pier in Dutch Harbor, Unalaska, amid a world of green hills and meadows like those at Kadiak. It was warm and cloudy, with light rain. We tarried here half a day, taking in coal and water, visiting the old Russian town of Iliuliuk a couple of miles away at the head of another indentation in the harbor, strolling through the wild meadows, or climbing the emerald heights.

One new bird, the Lapland longspur, which in color, flight, and song suggested our bobolink, at-

tracted our attention here. As we came " cross lots "
over the flower-besprinkled, undulating plain from
the old town to the new, this bird was in song all
about us, hovering in the air, pouring out its liquid,
bubbling song, and dropping down in the grass
again in a way very suggestive of the home bird, —
so much so that it may be fitly called the northland
bobolink.

TO THE LAPLAND LONGSPUR

Oh! thou northland bobolink,
   Looking over summer's brink,
Up to winter, worn and dim,
   Peering down from mountain rim,
Peering out on Bering Sea,
   To higher lands where he may flee, —
Something takes me in thy note,
   Quivering wing and bubbling throat,
Something moves me in thy ways, —
   Bird, rejoicing in thy days,
In thy upward hovering flight,
   In thy suit of black and white,
Chestnut cape and circled crown,
   In thy mate of speckled brown ;
Surely I may pause and think
   Of my boyhood's bobolink.

Soaring over meadows wild, —
   (Greener pastures never smiled)

FAR AND NEAR

Raining music from above, —
   Full of rapture, full of love ;
Frolic, gay, and debonair,
   Yet not all exempt from care,
For thy nest is in the grass,
   And thou worriest as I pass ;
But no hand nor foot of mine
   Shall do harm to thee or thine ;
I, musing, only pause to think
   Of my boyhood's bobolink.

But no bobolink of mine
   Ever sang o'er mead so fine, —
Starred with flowers of every hue,
   Gold and purple, white and blue.
Painted cup, anemone,
   Jacob's ladder, fleur-de-lis,
Orchid, harebell, shooting-star,
   Crane's bill, lupine, seen afar,
Primrose, rubus, saxifrage,
   Pictured type on Nature's page, —
These and others, here unnamed,
   In northland gardens, yet untamed,
Deck the fields where thou dost sing,
   Mounting up on trembling wing ;
Yet in wistful mood I think
   Of my boyhood's bobolink.

On Unalaska's emerald lea,
   On lonely isles in Bering Sea,

On far Siberia's barren shore,
  On north Alaska's tundra floor ;
At morn, at noon, in pallid night,
  We heard thy song and saw thy flight,
While I, sighing, could but think
  Of my boyhood's bobolink.

On the higher peaks, amid lingering snow-banks,
Mr. Ridgway found the snow bunting and the titlark nesting. Unalaska looked quite as interesting as
Kadiak, and I longed to spend some days there in
the privacy of its green solitudes, following its limpid
trout streams, climbing its lofty peaks, and listening to the music of the longspur. I had seen much,
but had been intimate with little ; now if I could
only have a few days of that kind of intimacy with
this new nature which the saunterer, the camper-
out, the stroller through fields in the summer twilight has, I should be more content; but in the afternoon the ship was off into Bering Sea, headed for
the Seal Islands, and I was aboard her, but with
wistful and reverted eyes.

The first hour or two out from Dutch Harbor we
sailed past high, rolling, green hills, cut squarely off
by the sea, presenting cliffs seven or eight hundred
feet high of soft, reddish, crumbling rock, a kind of
clay porphyry of volcanic origin, touched here and
there on the face with the tenderest green. It was as
if some green fluid had been poured upon the tops of

101

the hills, and had run down and dripped off the rock eaves and been caught upon every shelf and projection. The color was deepest in all the wrinkles and folds of the slopes and in the valley bottoms. At one point we looked into a deep, smooth valley or trough opening upon the sea, its shore-line a complete half-circle. Its bottom was nearly at the water level, and was as fresh and vivid as a lawn in spring. Some one suggested that it looked like a huge dry dock, if dry docks are ever carpeted with grass. The effect was extremely strange and beautiful. The clouds rested low across the hills, and formed a dense canopy over the vast verdant cradle; under this canopy we looked along a soft green vista for miles back into the hills, where patches of snow were visible. At another point a similar trough or cradle had been carved down to within a hundred or more feet of the sea, and upon its rocky face hung a beautiful waterfall. Then followed other lesser valleys that did not show the same glacial cross-section; they were V-shaped instead of U-shaped, each marked by a waterfall into the sea. There were three of these in succession cutting the rocky sea front into pyramidal forms. Often the talus at the foot of the cliffs was touched by the same magic green. Then opened up larger valleys, into which we looked under an up-rolled drop-curtain of cloud. One of them, lighted up by the sun, showed us an irregularly carved valley landscape, suggesting endless possibilities of flocks

102

and herds and rural homes. Here again the green
fluid seemed to have found its way down the creases
and runnels and was deepest there. Everywhere
such a sweep of green skirts as these Alaskan hills
and mountains present, often trailing to the sea!
I never tired of them, and if I dwell upon them
unduly long, let the reader remember that a thousand miles of this kind of scenery, passing slowly
before one on a succession of summer days, make
an impression not easily thrown off.

THE SEAL ISLANDS

Before many hours we ran into lowering, misty
weather in Bering Sea, and about seven o'clock were
off the Bogoslof Islands, two abrupt volcanic
mounds, one of them thrown up in recent years. The
other is the breeding-ground of innumerable sea-
lions, yes, and of myriads of murres, a species of
diver. With our glasses, when we were several miles
away, we could see the murres making the air almost
thick about the rocks as with clouds of black specks.
We could see the sea-lions, too, great windrows of
them, upon the beach. We dropped anchor about
two miles away, and a party of seven or eight went
ashore in a boat, — a hazardous proceeding, our captain thought, as the fog seemed likely to drop at any
moment and obliterate island and ship alike; but it
did not drop, only the top of the island was oblit-
erated. We could see the sea-lions lift themselves up

103

and gather in groups as the boat approached their rookery.

Then, after the landing was effected, they disappeared, and we could see the spray rise up as the monsters plunged into the water. Hundreds of them were in a small lake a few rods back from the shore, and the spectacle which the procession of the huge creatures made rushing across the beach to the sea was described as something most extraordinary. Those who were so fortunate as to witness it placed it among the three or four most memorable events of their lives.

On the afternoon of Sunday, July 9, we dropped anchor off St. Paul Island, one of the Pribilofs, the famous resort of the fur seals. A special permit from the Secretary of the Treasury gave us the privilege. There is no harbor here, and the landing, even in calm weather, requires to be carefully managed. The island is low, with a fringe of loose boulders around it, which in places looked almost like an artificial wall. The government agent conducted us a mile or more through wild meadows starred with flowers and covered with grass nearly knee-high, to the boulder-paved shore where the seals were congregated. Those of our party who had been there before, not many years back, were astonished at the diminished numbers of the animals, — hardly one tenth of the earlier myriads. We visited eight or ten "harems," as they are called, groups of a dozen or

104

more females, each presided over by a male or bull seal, whose position was usually upon a kind of throne or higher boulder in the midst of his wives. Every few minutes this male, which was much larger and darker in color than the females, would lift himself up and glance around over his circle as if counting his flock, then snarl at some rival a few yards away, or turn and threaten us. We gazed upon them and trained our cameras at leisure. Often a young male, wifeless and crowded back by older bulls, threatened us near the edge of the grass with continued demonstrations of anger. These unmated males were in bad humor anyway, and our appearance seemed to furnish them a good excuse to give vent to their feelings. In this market the females belong to the strong. We saw several forlorn old males hovering around, who had played the game and lost. They looked like bankrupt gamblers at a watering-place.

The females are much smaller and lighter in color than their lords and masters. They lay very quietly among the rocks, now and then casting uneasy glances at us. Their heads are small and their jaws slender; their growls and threats are not very terrifying.

Lying there in masses or wriggling about upon the rocks, all their lines soft and flowing, all their motions hampered, the fur seals suggest huge larvæ, or something between the grub and the mature insect. They appear to be yet in a kind of sac or envelope. The males wriggle about like a man in a bag; but once in the water, they are a part of the wave, as fleet and nimble as a fish, or as a bird in the air. In the sounds which they continually emitted they did not remind me of bulls or cows, but of sheep. The hoarse staccato bleating of the males was like that of old rams, while the shriller calls of the females and the fine treble of the pups were equally like those of ewes and lambs. Some belated females were still arriving while we looked on. They came in timidly, lifted themselves upon the edge of the rocks, and looked about as if to find a vacant place, or to receive a welcome. Much sparring and threatening were going on among the males, but I saw none actually come to blows. By careful movements and low tones we went about without much exciting them.

On this island we first saw the yellow poppy. It was scattered everywhere amid the grass, like the scarlet poppy of Europe. A wonderful display of other wild flowers was about our feet as we walked. Here also the Lapland longspur was in song, and a few snow buntings in white plumage drifted about over the flowery meads. On a big windrow of boulders along the beach near where we landed were swarms of noisy water-birds, mainly least auklets, called " choochkies " by the natives.

SIBERIA

According to our original programme our outward journey should have ended at the Seal Islands, but Mrs. Harriman expressed a wish to see Siberia, and, if all went well, the midnight sun. "Very well," replied Mr. Harriman, "we will go to Siberia," and toward that barren shore our prow was turned. It was about eight o'clock in the evening when we left St. Paul; a dense fog prevailed, hiding the shore. We had not been an hour under way when a horrible raking blow from some source made the ship tremble from stem to stern; then another and another, still more severe. The shock came from beneath: our keel was upon the rocks. Many of the company were at dinner; all sprang to their feet, and looked the surprise and alarm they did not speak. The engines were quickly reversed, a sail was hoisted; in a few moments the ship's prow swung off to the right, and the danger was passed, — we were afloat again. The stern of the ship, which was two feet deeper in the water than the bow, had raked across the rocks. No damage was done, and we had had a novel sensation, something analogous, I fancy, to the feeling one has upon land during an earthquake.

Some of us hoped this incident would cause Mr. Harriman to turn back. Bering Sea is a treacherous sea; it is shallow; it has many islands; and in sum-

mer it is nearly always draped in fog. Our host was
a man not easy to turn back, and in five minutes he
was romping with his children again as if nothing
had happened. The ship's course was changed to
southeast, around Walrus Island ; and it did, indeed,
look for a while as if we had more than half a mind
to turn back ; but in a couple of hours we were
headed toward Siberia again, and went plunging
through the fog and obscurity with our "ferocious
whistle," as Professor Emerson characterized it,
tearing the silence and our sleep alike to tatters.
The next day, the 10th, we hoped to touch at the
Island of St. Matthew, but we missed it in the thick
obscurity and searching for it was hazardous, so we
went again northward.

The fog continued on the 11th till nearly noon,
when we ran into clear air and finally into sunshine,
and in the early afternoon the coast of Siberia lay
before us like a cloud upon the horizon, — Asia at
last, crushed down there on the rim of the world as
though with the weight of her centuries and her cruel
Czar's iniquities. As we drew near, her gray, crumbling, decrepit granite bluffs and mountains, streaked
with snow, helped the illusion. This was the Old
World indeed. Our destination was Plover Bay,
where at six in the afternoon we dropped anchor
behind a long, crescent-shaped sandspit that put
out from the eastern shore. On this sandspit was an
Eskimo encampment of skin-covered huts, which

was soon astir with moving forms. Presently eight of the figures were seen moving down to the beach. A boat was launched and filled, and came rapidly to the ship's side. It was made of walrus skin stretched over a wooden frame, and was a strong, shapely craft. Its occupants also were clad in skins. There were three women and nine men in the boat, but one had to look very closely to tell which was which. The men's crowns were shaved, leaving a heavy fringe of coarse black hair around their heads. One of them, probably thirty or thirty-five years of age, stood up in the bow of the boat, and with his cloak of reddish-gray fur was really a handsome man. He had a thin black beard and regular, clear-cut features, and looked as one fancies an old Roman of his age might have looked. They were evidently drawn to us partly by curiosity and partly by the hope of gifts of tobacco and whiskey. The tobacco was freely showered upon them by Mr. Harriman, and was eagerly seized, but the whiskey was not forthcoming.

Our own boats were rapidly lowered, and we were soon upon Asiatic soil, gathering flowers, observing the birds, and strolling about among the tents and huts of the natives. We bought skins and curios of them, or bartered knives and cloth for such things as they had to dispose of. They would take our silver dollars, but much preferred skinning-knives or other useful articles. They were not shy of our cameras, and freely admitted us to the greasy and smoky interiors of their dwellings. As the Eskimos stood regarding us, they would draw their hands into their sleeves, after the manner of children on a cold morning. Their skin costumes gave them a singular stuffed appearance. One was reminded of grotesque dolls filled with bran or sawdust. This effect was due in part to the awkward cut of their garments and to the fact that the skins were made up hair side in. Some of the natives showed a strain of European blood; whalers bound for the Arctic Ocean sometimes stop here, and corrupt them with bad morals and villainous whiskey.

Throughout the village seals and seal oil, reindeer skins, walrus hides, and blubber were most noticeable. Behind the tent I saw a deep, partly covered pit in the ground, nearly filled with oil, and a few rods farther off others were seen. The bones of whales served instead of timbers in most of the rude structures. The winter houses were built by standing up whale ribs about two feet apart in a circle, and filling up the interstices with turf, making a wall two feet thick. For a roof they used walrus hides, resting upon poles. In my walk over this crescent of land I came here and there upon the huge vertebræ of whales, scattered about, and looking like the gray, weather-worn granite boulders on a New England farm.

Beyond the present site of the encampment I saw

the ruins of an older or earlier village, the foundations of whale bones partly overgrown by the turf.

As we came in at one end of the encampment most of the dogs went out at the other end. They had never before seen such looking creatures, and they fled off toward the mountain, where they sat down and howled their mournful protest. Some of the children were frightened too; one youngster of five or six years, stuffed like a small scarecrow, riding astride his mother's neck, cried and yelled vigorously as we approached. The sun was bright, but the air was very chilly, the mercury standing at about 38° Fahrenheit. We were within one hundred and twenty miles of the Arctic circle. The slender peninsula we were on was a few hundred feet wide; it was marshy in some places, but for the most part dry and covered with herbage. Here were yellow poppies blooming, and two species of saxifrage. In my walk I came upon a large patch of ground covered with a small, low, pink primrose. The ground was painted with it. But the prettiest flower we found was a forget-me-not, scarcely an inch high, of deep ultramarine blue, — the deepest, most intense blue I ever saw in a wild flower. Here also we saw and heard the Lapland longspur and the yellow wagtail. A flock of male eider ducks was seen in the bay.

111

FAR AND NEAR

We traveled two hours in Asia. I am tempted to write a book on the country, but forbear. At eight o'clock we steamed away along the coast toward Indian Point, in an unending twilight. We arrived there at midnight, but the surf was running so high that no landing was attempted. Then we stood off across Bering Strait for Port Clarence in Alaska, where we hoped to take water, passing in sight of King Island and the Diomedes, and about noon again dropped anchor behind a long, sickle-shaped sandspit, which curves out from the southern head-land, ten or twelve miles away. In the great basin behind this sand-bar a dozen vessels of the whaling fleet were anchored and making ready to enter the Arctic Ocean, where some of them expected to spend the winter. The presence of the fleet had drawn to-gether upon the sand-bar over two hundred Eskimos for trade and barter with the whalers. Their shapely skin boats, filled with people, — men, women, chil-dren, often to the number of twenty, to say nothing of the dogs, — soon swarmed about our ship. They had all manner of furs, garments, baskets, ornaments, and curios for sale or for barter. An animated and picturesque scene they presented, and dozens of cameras were leveled at them. In dress they pre-sented a much more trim and shapely appearance than did the people we had just left in Siberia, though

112

much the same in other respects. Some of the younger women were fairly good-looking, and their fur hoods and fur cloaks became them well. I noticed that the babies cried very much as babies do at home. Most of the women were dressed in hair seal or reindeer skins, but some wore an outer garment of colored cotton cloth, hanging loosely to the knees. It was interesting to see them tuck their babies under this garment from the rear. The mother would bend forward very low, thrust the child under the garment at her hips, and by a dexterous wriggling movement of her body propel it forward till its head protruded above her shoulder. One marked its course along her back as he does that of a big morsel down a chicken's gullet.

Some of the captains of the whalers came aboard our ship to advise us about taking water. They were large, powerful, resolute-looking men, quite equal, one would say, to the task before them. Water was to be procured from a stream that ran in from the tundra on the southern shore of the bay about a dozen miles distant. Leaving part of our company to visit the whalers and the Eskimos, the ship steamed away with the rest of us for water, and in due course anchored near the mouth of the little stream. This gave us an opportunity to spend several hours upon the real tundra. Cape Nome was on the other side of the peninsula, fifty miles away, but the fame of the gold fields had not then reached us. We may have

113

walked over ground rich in gold, but our mining expert failed to call our attention to the fact. As we approached the land, it looked as smooth as if it had just been gone over with a mowing-machine. My first thought was, "Well, the people are done haying here." The tundra was of a greenish brown color, and rose from a long, crescent-shaped beach in a very gentle ascent to low cones and bare volcanic peaks many miles away. It had the appearance of a vast meadow tilted up but a few degrees from the level. This, then, was the tundra that covers so much of North America, where the ground remains perpetually frozen to an unknown depth, thawing out only a foot or so on the surface during the summer. How eagerly we stepped upon it; how quickly we dispersed in all directions, lured on by the strangeness ! In a few moments our hands were full of wild flowers, which we kept dropping to gather others more attractive, these, in turn, to be discarded as still more novel ones appeared. I found myself very soon treading upon a large pink claytonia or spring beauty, many times the size of our delicate April flower of the same name. Soon I came upon a bank by the little creek covered with a low, nodding purple primrose; then masses of the shooting-star attracted me ; then several species of pedicularis, a yellow anemone, and many saxifrages. A complete list of flowers blooming here within sixty miles of the Arctic circle, in a thin layer of soil resting upon perpetual frost, would be a long one. There were wild bees here too, to cross-fertilize the flowers, and bumble-bees boomed by very much as at home. And mosquitoes, how they swarmed up out of the grass upon me when, in my vain effort to reach a little volcanic cone that rose up there before me like a haystack in a meadow, I sat down to rest! I could not seem to get nearer the haystack, though I sometimes ran to get away from the mosquitoes. The tundra proved far less smooth to the feet than the eye had promised. It was wet and boggy. A tundra is always wet in summer, as the frost prevents any underground drainage. But it was very uniform and the walking not difficult; moss, bogs, grass, and flowering plants covered it everywhere. The savanna sparrow and the longspur started up before me as I walked, and as I descended toward a branch of the little creek after an hour's tramp, a new note caught my ear. Presently I saw some plovers skimming over the ground in advance of me, or alighting upon tussocks of moss and uttering a soft, warbling call. They proved to be golden plovers; I had evidently invaded their breeding-grounds, and they were making their musical protest. At times the males, as they circled about me, warbled in the most delightful manner. There was in it, underneath its bright joyousness, a tone of soft pleading and entreaty that was very moving, — the voice of the tundra, soft, alluring, plaintive, beautiful. The golden plover is mottled black and white with a rich golden tinge on its back. It is a wonderful flyer. We found it near the Arctic circle; six months later, probably the same birds might have been found in Patagonia.

In a patch of willows along the creek the gray-cheeked thrush was in song, and the fox sparrow and the western tree sparrow were found. I saw one of the thrushes do what I never saw any of the thrush kind do before: it hovered in the air fifty feet or more above the moor and repeated its song three times very rapidly. As there were no trees to afford it a lofty perch, it perched upon the air.

It was a very novel experience, this walking over the tundra; its vastness, its uniformity, its solitude, its gentleness, its softness of contour, its truly boreal character, — the truncated hills and peaks on the near horizon suggesting huge earthworks, the rounded and curved elevations like the backs of prostrate giants turned up to the sun, and farther off the high, serrated, snow-streaked ranges on the remote horizon to the north, — all made up a curious and unfamiliar picture.

We were fortunate in having clear, bright skies during our stay in these high latitudes. But the nights were starless; the sun was so near, there was so much light in the sky, that the stars were put out. The sun set about ten and rose about two, dipping down but a little way below the horizon.

116

IN GREEN ALASKA

Port Clarence was the northernmost point we reached. A little farther north the ice pack closed the gateway to the Arctic Ocean. An excursion into the ice to see the midnight sun did not hold out inducements enough to offset the dangers. So in the early morning of July 13 we steamed away on the return trip. Before noon we were again in the thick veil of fog with which Bering Sea always seems to cover her face. Near nightfall, with a stiff wind blowing, we anchored off St. Lawrence Island, and two boat-loads of our people went ashore. St. Lawrence is a large island at the gateway of the Arctic Ocean, and in spring the ice floes from the north often strand polar bears upon it. Our hunters still dreamed of bears. The shore was low and marshy, and the high land miles away was hidden by the canopy of fog resting upon it. In his walk one of our doctors saw the backs of two large white objects, showing above a little swell in the land. Here evidently were the polar bears they were in quest of.

The doctor begins to stalk them, replacing the shells in his gun with heavier ones as he creeps along. Now he has another glimpse of the white backs; they are moving and can be nothing but bears. A few moments more and he will be within close range, when lo! the heads and long necks of two white swans come up above the bank! The doctor said he

117

never felt so much like a goose before in his life. The birds and flowers found were about the same as those we had already seen.

Not many years ago there were on St. Lawrence Island many encampments of Eskimos, embracing several hundred people. Late one autumn some whalers turned up there with the worst kind of whis-key, with which they wrought the ruin of the na-tives, persuading them to exchange most of their furs and other valuables for it, and leaving them so debauched and demoralized that nearly all perished of cold and hunger the following winter. Village after village was found quite depopulated, the people lying dead in their houses.

HALL AND ST. MATTHEW ISLANDS

From St. Lawrence Island our course was again through fog to St. Matthew Island, which we missed on our way up, and which we now found late in the afternoon of the next day. Our first stop was at Hall Island, which once probably formed a part of St. Matthew, but is now separated from it only by a nar-row strait. This was our first visit to uninhabited land, and to a land of such unique grace and beauty that the impression it made cannot soon be forgotten, — a thick carpet of moss and many-colored flowers covering an open, smooth, undulating country that faced the sea in dark basaltic cliffs, some of them a thousand feet high. The first thing that attracted

118

our attention was the murres — "arries," the Aleuts call them — about their rookeries on the cliffs. Their numbers darkened the air. As we approached, the faces of the rocks seemed paved with them, with a sprinkling of gulls, puffins, black cormorants, and auklets. On landing at a break in the cliffs where a little creek came down to the sea, our first impulse was to walk along the brink and look down upon the murres and see them swarm out beneath our feet. On the discharge of a gun the air became black with them, while the cliffs apparently remained as populous as ever. They sat on little shelves or niches with their black backs to the sea, each bird covering one egg with its tail feathers. In places one could have reached down and seized them by the neck, they were so tame and so near the top of the rocks. I believe one of our party did actually thus procure a specimen. It was a strange spectacle, and we lingered long looking upon it. To behold sea fowl like flies in uncounted millions was a new experience. Everywhere in Bering Sea the murres swarm like vermin. It seems as if there was a murre to every square yard of surface. They were flying about over the ship or flapping over the water away from her front at all times. I noticed that they could not get up from the water except against the wind; the wind lifted them as it does a kite. With the wind or in a calm they skimmed along on the surface, their heads bent forward, their wings beating the water impatiently.

119

Unable to rise, they would glance behind them in a frightened manner, then plunge beneath the waves until they thought the danger had passed. At all hours of the night and day one could hear this impatient flapping of the frightened murres. The bird is a species of diver, nearly as large as a black duck. Its tail is so short that in flying the two webbed feet stretched behind do the duty of a tail. It is amusing to see it spread or contract them in turning or changing its course, as the case requires. After we had taken our fill of gazing upon the murres came the ramble away from the cliffs, in the long twilight, through that mossy and flowery solitude. Such patterns and suggestions for rugs and carpets as we walked over for hours; such a blending of grays, drabs, browns, greens, and other delicate neutral tints, all dashed with masses of many-colored flowers, it had never before been my fortune to behold, much less to walk upon. Drifting over this marvelous carpet, or dropping down upon it from the air above, was the hyperborean snowbird, white as a snowflake and with a song of great sweetness and power. With lifted wings the bird would drop through the air to the earth, pouring out its joyous, ecstatic strain. Out of the deep twilight came also the song of the longspur, delivered on the wing, and touching the wild solitude like the voices of children at play. Then there was the large Aleutian sandpiper, that ran before me and uttered its curious wild

120

plaint. The robber jaeger was there too, — a very beautiful bird, a sort of cross between a hawk and a gull, — sitting quietly upon the moss and eying our movements. On the top of the grassy bank near the sea some of the party found the nest and young of the snowy owl. Fragments of the bodies of murres and ducks lay upon the ground beside it.

The most novel and striking of the wild flowers was a species of large white claytonia growing in rings of the size of a tea plate, floral rings dropped here and there upon the carpet of moss. In the centre was a rosette of pointed green leaves pressed close to the ground; around this grew the ring of flowers, made up of thirty or forty individuals, all springing from the same root, their faces turned out in all directions from the parent centre. In places they were so near together that one could easily step from one circle to another.

The forenoon of the next day, the 15th, we spent upon St. Matthew Island, and repeated our experience of walking over ground covered with nature's matchless tapestry. Here, too, a thick, heavy carpet of variegated mosses and lichens had been stretched to the very edge of the cliffs, with rugs and mats of many-colored flowers — pink, yellow, violet, white; saxifrage, chickweed, astragalus, claytonia — dropped here and there upon it. Sometimes the flowers seemed worked into the carpet itself, and a species of creeping willow spread its leaves out as if stitched upon it. Scattered about were the yellow poppies, a yellow and a red pedicularis, and a rare and curious blue flower in heads, the name of which I have forgotten. On the highest point the blue and purple astragalus covered large areas, but the most novel of all the flowers was a species of little silene with a bluish ribbed flower precisely like a miniature Chinese lantern.

The highest point of the island was enveloped most of the time in fog and cloud. While groping my way upon one of these cloud summits, probably a thousand feet above the sea which flowed at its base, I came suddenly upon a deep cleft or chasm, which opened in the moss and flowers at my feet and led down between crumbling rocky walls at a fearful incline to the beach. It gave one a sense of peril that made him pause quickly. The wraiths of fog and mist whirling through and over it enhanced its dreadful mystery and depth. Yet I hovered about it, retreating and returning, quite fascinated by the contrast between the smooth flowery carpet upon which I stood and the terrible yawning chasm. When the fog lifted a little and the sun gleamed out, I looked down this groove into the ocean, and Tennyson's line came to mind as accurately descriptive of the scene: —

" The wrinkled sea beneath him crawls."

Another curious effect was the appearance of the

bottom of the sea, visible a long way out from shore. The water seemed suddenly to become shallow or else to take on a strange transparency; the color and configuration of the rocky floor were surprisingly distinct.

A new species of small blue fox was found and killed upon the island, and a sorry apology for a fox it was.[1] It looked as though it might have been singed or else skinned once, and as though this was the second growth of fur. The polar bears which our sportsmen had hoped for were not found, though the deep, broad, unused trails leading back from the cliffs had doubtless some time been made by them. Nothing is plainer than that one cannot go to Alaska, or probably to any other country, and say, " Come, now, we will kill a bear," and kill it, except as a rare streak of luck. It is a game at which two can play, and the bear plays his part extremely well. All large game has its beat or range. The first thing to be done is to find this beat, which may take days or weeks, then the trial of strategy begins. If you outgeneral the bear, you may carry off his pelt.

We found the hyperborean snow bunting nesting in crevices of the rocks. It was probably compelled to this course to escape the foxes. This was the type locality for this bird, and it was very abundant. The rosy finch also was seen along the cliffs. There were

[1] This was the Hall Island Arctic fox (*Vulpes hallensis* Merriam) in worn summer dress; in winter it is snow white.

snow-banks on the beach by the sea, and piles of driftwood, most of the large tree trunks doubtless brought down by the Yukon, and many hewn and sawed timbers from wrecked vessels.

THE RETURN TRIP

Returning to Unalaska, we tarried a few hours at Dutch Harbor to take in water and coal, and then, for the first time, our good ship pointed eastward and toward home. A steamer from the Yukon was also in Dutch Harbor with several hundred returning gold-seekers on board. As we steamed away I saw several of them far up on the green mountain-side on our left looking down upon us. They were barely distinguishable on that broad, high, emerald slope. Just out of the harbor we saw myriads of fulmars, a kind of petrel. The sea for miles was black with them. We touched again at the Shumagin Islands to pick up the party we had left there on the 7th; and on the 20th were again at sweet pastoral Kadiak. The wild roses were in bloom, very large and fine, and armfuls of them were brought in to deck the table in celebration of the birthday of one of Mr. Harriman's daughters. While here we took an afternoon to visit Long Island, ten or twelve miles away, where there was another fox farm. It was a low, wooded island of several hundred acres stocked with about a thousand blue foxes. Some of the animals peeped shyly at us

AMERICAN MAGPIE

from around the corner of an old barn, others growled at us from beneath it, while others still lifted up their voices in protest from the woods. A great many fish, trout and salmon, were drying in the sun from poles on the beach in front. These were for the foxes in winter. Magpies were common here and very tame. The farmer had a comfortable home and a pleasant situation, and life there must have many attractions. The experiment of growing silver-black foxes had been tried, but had not succeeded. The animals were so wild, and proved to be such dainty feeders, that the undertaking was abandoned. They require live game for food.

On leaving Kadiak we again ran into Cook Inlet, and put ashore two parties. But there was a sudden change of plan, the parties were recalled, and we were soon again at sea, homeward bound.

ST. ELIAS AND THE FAIRWEATHER RANGE

On the 23d we had such a view of St. Elias and all that grand range as is seldom granted to voyagers. One of our artists, Mr. Gifford, was up at two o'clock in the morning, and finding the summit just smitten with the rising sun, painted till his hands were too cold to hold the brush.

We again ran into Yakutat Bay, but all I have to record is our feast of Yakutat strawberries. The Indians brought them to us in baskets. The berries looked pale and uninviting, but their flavor was really excellent. They grow in great abundance in the sand on the beach. On the 24th we steamed all day off the Fairweather Range, which lay there before us without a cloud or film to dim its naked majesty. We were two or three hours in passing the great peak itself. Piled with snow and beaten upon by a cloudless sun, its reflected light shone in my stateroom like that of an enormous full moon. This was a day in blue and white, — blue of the sea and sky and white of the mountains, — long to be remembered but not to be described. The peak of St. Elias, standing above a band of cloud, kept us in its eye till we were one hundred and fifty miles down the coast.

On the 25th we were at Juneau again, taking coal and water. The only toad I saw in Alaska I saw this day, as it was fumbling along in the weeds by the roadside, just out of Juneau. Here also I gathered my first salmon-berries, — a kind of raspberry an inch in diameter, with a slightly bitterish flavor, but very good.

The lovely weather still favored us on our return trip down the inland passage. Under date of the 26th I find this entry in my note-book: —

"Bright and warm and still; all day down the inside passage. At one point in Tongass Narrows, fishermen taking salmon: a large seine gathered in between two rowboats, one of them bright red, and men in each with forks picking the fish out of the net and throwing them into the boat. The salmon glance and wriggle in the sun like bars of silver. Bristling forests, tufted islands, snow-striped peaks on every side. A soft, placid day, when nature broods and dreams, both sea and shore wrapped in a profound midsummer tranquillity."

In the afternoon we anchored off a deserted Indian village north of Cape Fox. There was a row of a dozen houses on the beach of a little bay, with nineteen totem poles standing along their fronts. These totem poles were the attraction. There was a rumor that the Indians had nearly all died of small-pox a few years before, and that the few survivors had left under a superstitious fear, never to return. It was evident that the village had not been occupied for seven or eight years. Why not, therefore, secure some of these totem poles for the museums of the various colleges represented by members of the expedition? This was finally agreed upon, and all hands, including the ship's crew, fell to digging up and floating to the ship five or six of the more striking poles. This occupied us till the night of the 27th.

Under this date I find this entry in my note-book: " All day on shore by the deserted Indian village. Clear and hot. I sit in the shade of the spruces amid huge logs of driftwood on the upper edge of the beach, with several Indian graves at my back, under the trees, and write up my notes, — the ship at anchor out in the bay a mile away. Aided by the sailors the men are taking down totem poles and towing them to the ship with the naphtha launches. As I write there are many birds in the trees and bushes near me, — the rufous hummer, the rufous-backed chickadee, the golden-crowned kinglet, the pine siskin. Back in the woods I hear the russet-backed thrush and Steller's jay. With my lunch I have some salmon-berries gathered near by."

"July 28. Woke up this morning hearing the birds sing through my open window. I looked out into the dusky wooded side of a mountain nearly within a stone's throw. We were in Grenville Channel, the skies clear, the sun shining full upon the opposite shore. Presently we were passing one of those bewitching alcoves or recesses in the shore where the mountains form a loop miles deep around an inlet of blue sea, with snow-crowned peaks above great curves of naked rock at the head of it. Then we cut one of those curious tide-lines, where two currents of water of different colors meet. The dividing line is sharp and clear for a long distance."

The next day, which was still bright and warm, there was a film of smoke in the air in the morning, which increased as we went south. We were nearing the region of forest fires. When we reached Seattle on July 30, this smoke had so increased that all the great mountains were hidden by it as effectually as they had been by the clouds when we entered upon the voyage.

We had three tons of coal left in our bunkers, but of our little stock farm down below only the milch cow remained. She had been to Siberia and back, and had given milk all the way.

No voyagers were ever more fortunate than we. No storms, no winds, no delays nor accidents to speak of, no illness. We had gone far and fared well.

II

WILD LIFE ABOUT MY CABIN

FRIENDS have often asked me why I turned my back upon the Hudson and retreated into the wilderness. Well, I do not call it a retreat; I call it a withdrawal, a retirement, the taking up of a new position to renew the attack, it may be, more vigorously than ever. It is not always easy to give reasons. There are reasons within reasons, and often no reasons at all that we are aware of.

To a countryman like myself, not born to a great river or an extensive water-view, these things, I think, grow wearisome after a time. He becomes surfeited with a beauty that is alien to him. He longs for something more homely, private, and secluded. Scenery may be too fine or too grand and imposing for one's daily and hourly view. It tires after a while. It demands a mood that comes to you only at intervals. Hence it is never wise to build your house on the most ambitious spot in the landscape. Rather seek out a more humble and secluded nook or corner, which you can fill and warm with your domestic and home instincts and affections. In some things the half is often more satisfying than the whole. A

131

glimpse of the Hudson River between hills or through openings in the trees wears better with me than a long expanse of it constantly spread out before me. One day I had an errand to a farmhouse nestled in a little valley or basin at the foot of a mountain. The earth put out protecting arms all about it, — a low hill with an orchard on one side, a sloping pasture on another, and the mountain, with the skirts of its mantling forests, close at hand in the rear. How my heart warmed toward it! I had been so long perched high upon the banks of a great river, in sight of all the world, exposed to every wind that blows, with a horizon-line that sweeps over half a county, that, quite unconsciously to myself, I was pining for a nook to sit down in. I was hungry for the private and the circumscribed; I knew it when I saw this sheltered farmstead. I had long been restless and dissatisfied, — a vague kind of homesickness; now I knew the remedy. Hence when, not long afterward, I was offered a tract of wild land, barely a mile from home, that contained a secluded nook and a few acres of level, fertile land shut off from the vain and noisy world of railroads, steamboats, and yachts by a wooded, precipitous mountain, I quickly closed the bargain, and built me a rustic house there, which I call "Slabsides," because its outer walls are covered with slabs. I might have given it a prettier name, but not one more fit, or more in keeping with the mood that brought me thither.

A slab is the first cut from the log, and the bark goes with it. It is like the first cut from the loaf, which we call the crust, and which the children reject, but which we older ones often prefer. I wanted to take a fresh cut of life, — something that had the bark on, or, if you please, that was like a well-browned and hardened crust. After three years I am satisfied with the experiment. Life has a different flavor here. It is reduced to simpler terms; its complex equations all disappear. The exact value of x may still elude me, but I can press it hard; I have shorn it of many of its disguises and entanglements.

When I went into the woods the robins went with me, or rather they followed close. As soon as a space of ground was cleared and the garden planted, they were on hand to pick up the worms and insects, and to superintend the planting of the cherry-trees: three pairs the first summer, and more than double that number the second. In the third, their early morning chorus was almost as marked a feature as it is about the old farm homesteads. The robin is no hermit: he likes company; he likes the busy scenes of the farm and the village; he likes to carol to listening ears, and to build his nest as near your dwelling as he can. Only at rare intervals do I find a real sylvan robin, one that nests in the woods, usually by still waters, remote from human habitation. In such places his morning and evening carol is a welcome surprise to the fisherman or camper-out. It is like a dooryard flower found blooming in the wilderness. With the robins came the song sparrows and social sparrows, or chippies, also. The latter nested in the bushes near my cabin, and the song sparrows in the bank above the ditch that drains my land. I notice that Chippy finds just as many horsehairs to weave into her nest here in my horseless domain as she does when she builds in the open country. Her partiality for the long hairs from the manes and tails of horses and cattle is so great that she is often known as the hair-bird. What would she do in a country where there were neither cows nor horses? Yet these hairs are not good nesting-material. They are slippery, refractory things, and occasionally cause a tragedy in the nest by getting looped around the legs or the neck of the young or of the parent bird. They probably give a smooth finish to the interior, dear to the heart of Chippy.

The first year of my cabin life a pair of robins attempted to build a nest upon the round timber that forms the plate under my porch roof. But it was a poor place to build in. It took nearly a week's time and caused the birds a great waste of labor to find this out. The coarse material they brought for the foundation would not bed well upon the rounded surface of the timber, and every vagrant breeze that came along swept it off. My porch was kept littered with twigs and weed-stalks for days, till finally the birds abandoned the undertaking. The next season a wiser or more experienced pair made the attempt again, and succeeded. They placed the nest against the rafter where it joins the plate; they used mud from the start to level up with and to hold the first twigs and straws, and had soon completed a firm, shapely structure. When the young were about ready to fly, it was interesting to note that there was apparently an older and a younger, as in most families. One bird was more advanced than any of the others. Had the parent birds intentionally stimulated it with extra quantities of food, so as to be able to launch their offspring into the world one at a time? At any rate, one of the birds was ready to leave the nest a day and a half before any of the others. I happened to be looking at it when the first impulse to get outside the nest seemed to seize it. Its parents were encouraging it with calls and assurances from some rocks a few yards away. It answered their calls in vigorous, strident tones. Then it climbed over the edge of the nest upon the plate, took a few steps forward, then a few more, till it was a yard from the nest and near the end of the timber, and could look off into free space. Its parents apparently shouted, "Come on!" But its courage was not quite equal to the leap; it looked around, and seeing how far it was from home, scampered back to the nest, and climbed into it like a frightened child. It had made its first journey into the world, but the home tie had brought it quickly back.

A few hours afterward it journeyed to the end of the plate again, and then turned and rushed back. The third time its heart was braver, its wings stronger, and leaping into the air with a shout, it flew easily to some rocks a dozen or more yards away. Each of the young in succession, at intervals of nearly a day, left the nest in this manner. There would be the first journey of a few feet along the plate, the first sudden panic at being so far from home, the rush back, a second and perhaps a third attempt, and then the irrevocable leap into the air, and a clamorous flight to a near-by bush or rock. Young birds never go back when they have once taken flight. The first free flap of the wing severs forever the ties that bind them to home.

The chickadees we have always with us. They are like the evergreens among the trees and plants. Winter has no terrors for them. They are properly wood-birds, but the groves and orchards know them also. Did they come near my cabin for better protection, or did they chance to find a little cavity in a tree there that suited them ? Branch-builders and ground-builders are easily accommodated, but the chickadee must find a cavity, and a small one at that. The woodpeckers make a cavity when a suitable trunk or branch is found, but the chickadee, with its small, sharp beak, rarely does so; it usually smooths and deepens one already formed. This a pair did a few yards from my cabin. The opening

136

was into the heart of a little sassafras, about four feet from the ground. Day after day the birds took turns in deepening and enlarging the cavity: a soft, gentle hammering for a few moments in the heart of the little tree, and then the appearance of the worker at the opening, with the chips in his, or her, beak. They changed off every little while, one working while the other gathered food. Absolute equality of the sexes, both in plumage and in duties, seems to prevail among these birds, as among a few other species. During the preparations for housekeeping the birds were hourly seen and heard, but as soon as the first egg was laid, all this was changed. They suddenly became very shy and quiet. Had it not been for the new egg that was added each day, one would have concluded that they had abandoned the place. There was a precious secret now that must be well kept. After incubation began, it was only by watching that I could get a glimpse of one of the birds as it came quickly to feed or to relieve the other.

One day a lot of Vassar girls came to visit me, and I led them out to the little sassafras to see the chickadees' nest. The sitting bird kept her place as head after head, with its nodding plumes and millinery, appeared above the opening to her chamber, and a pair of inquisitive eyes peered down upon her. But I saw that she was getting ready to play her little trick to frighten them away. Presently I heard a faint explosion at the bottom of the cavity, when the peeping girl jerked her head quickly back, with the exclamation, "Why, it spit at me!" The trick of the bird on such occasions is apparently to draw in its breath till its form perceptibly swells, and then give forth a quick, explosive sound like an escaping jet of steam. One involuntarily closes his eyes and jerks back his head. The girls, to their great amusement, provoked the bird into this pretty outburst of her impatience two or three times. But as the ruse failed of its effect, the bird did not keep it up, but let the laughing faces gaze till they were satisfied.

There is only one other bird known to me that resorts to the same trick to scare away intruders, and that is the great crested flycatcher. As your head appears before the entrance to the cavity in which the mother bird is sitting, a sudden burst of escaping steam seems directed at your face, and your backward movement leaves the way open for the bird to escape, which she quickly does.

The chickadee is a prolific bird, laying from six to eight eggs, and it seems to have few natural enemies. I think it is seldom molested by squirrels or black snakes or weasels or crows or owls. The entrance to the nest is usually so small that none of these creatures can come at them. Yet the number of chickadees in any given territory seems small. What keeps them in check ? Probably the rigors of winter and a limited food-supply. The ant-eaters, fruit-eaters, and seed-eaters mostly migrate. Our all-the-year-round birds, like the chickadees, wood-peckers, jays, and nuthatches, live mostly on nuts and the eggs and larvæ of tree-insects, and hence their larder is a restricted one; hence, also, these birds rear only one brood in a season. A hairy wood-pecker passed the winter in the woods near me by subsisting on a certain small white grub which he found in the bark of some dead hemlock-trees. He "worked" these trees, — four of them, — as the slang is, "for all they were worth." The grub was under the outer shell of bark, and the bird literally skinned the trees in getting at his favorite morsel. He worked from the top downward, hammering or prying off this shell, and leaving the trunk of the tree with a red, denuded look. Bushels of the frag-ments of the bark covered the ground at the foot of the tree in spring, and the trunk looked as if it had been flayed, — as it had.

The big chimney of my cabin of course attracted the chimney swifts, and as it was not used in sum-mer, two pairs built their nests in it, and we had the muffled thunder of their wings at all hours of the day and night. One night, when one of the broods was nearly fledged, the nest that held them fell down into the fireplace. Such a din of screeching and chattering as they instantly set up! Neither my dog nor I could sleep. They yelled in chorus, stop-ping at the end of every half-minute as if upon signal. Now they were all screeching at the top of their voices, then a sudden, dead silence ensued. Then the din began again, to terminate at the instant as before. If they had been long practicing together, they could not have succeeded better. I never before heard the cry of birds so accurately timed. After a while I got up and put them back up the chimney, and stopped up the throat of the flue with newspapers. The next day one of the parent birds, in bringing food to them, came down the chimney with such force that it passed through the papers and brought up in the fireplace. On capturing it I saw that its throat was distended with food as a chipmunk's cheek with corn, or a boy's pocket with chestnuts. I opened its mandibles, when it ejected a wad of insects as large as a bean. Most of them were much macerated, but there were two house-flies yet alive and but little the worse for their close confinement. They stretched themselves, and walked about upon my hand, enjoying a breath of fresh air once more. It was nearly two hours before the swift again ventured into the chimney with food.

These birds do not perch, nor alight upon buildings or the ground. They are apparently upon the wing all day. They outride the storms. I have in my mind a cheering picture of three of them I saw facing a heavy thunder-shower one afternoon. The wind was blowing a gale, the clouds were rolling in black, portentous billows out of the west, the peals of thunder were shaking the heavens, and the big drops were just beginning to come down, when, on looking up, I saw three swifts high in air, working their way slowly, straight into the teeth of the storm. They were not hurried or disturbed; they held themselves firmly and steadily; indeed, they were fairly at anchor in the air till the rage of the elements should have subsided. I do not know that any other of our land birds outride the storms in this way.

The phœbe-birds also soon found me out in my retreat, and a pair of them deliberated a long while about building on a little shelf in one of my gables. But, much to my regret, they finally decided in favor of a niche in the face of a ledge of rocks not far from my spring. The place was well screened by bushes and well guarded against the approach of snakes or four-footed prowlers, and the birds prospered well and reared two broods. They have now occupied the same nest three years in succession. This is unusual: Phœbe prefers a new nest each season, but in this case there is no room for another, and, the site being a choice one, she slightly repairs and refurnishes her nest each spring, leaving the new houses for her more ambitious neighbors.

Of wood-warblers my territory affords many specimens. One spring a solitary Nashville warbler lingered near my cabin for a week. I heard his bright, ringing song at all hours of the day. The next spring there were two or more, and they nested in my pea-bushes. The black and white creeping warblers are perhaps the most abundant. A pair of them built a nest in a steep moss and lichen covered hillside, beside a high gray rock. Our path to Julian's Rock led just above it. It was an ideal spot and an ideal nest, but it came to grief. Some small creature sucked the eggs. On removing the nest I found an earth-stained egg beneath it. Evidently the egg had ripened before its receptacle was ready, and the mother, for good luck, had placed it in the foundation.

One day, as I sat at my table writing, I had a call from the worm-eating warbler. It came into the open door, flitted about inquisitively, and then, startled by the apparition at the table, dashed against the window-pane and fell down stunned. I picked it up, and it lay with closed eyes panting in my hand. I carried it into the open air. In a moment or two it opened its eyes, looked about, and then closed them and fell to panting again. Soon it looked up at me once more and about the room, and seemed to say: " Where am I ? What has happened to me ? " Presently the panting ceased, the bird's breathing became more normal, it gradually got its bearings, and, at a motion of my hand, darted away. This is an abundant warbler in my vicinity, and nested this year near by. I have discovered that it has an air-song — the song of ecstasy — like that of the oven-bird. I had long suspected it, as I frequently heard a fine burst of melody that was new to me. One June day I was fortunate enough to see the bird delivering its song in the air above the low trees. As with the oven-bird, its favorite hour is the early twilight, though I hear the song occasionally at other hours. The bird darts upward fifty feet or more, about half the height that the oven-bird attains, and gives forth a series of rapid, ringing musical notes, which quickly glide into the long, sparrow-like trill that forms its ordinary workaday song. While this part is being uttered, the singer is on its downward flight into the woods. The flight-song of the oven-bird is louder and more striking, and is not so shy and furtive a performance. The latter I hear many times every June twilight, and I frequently see the singer reach his climax a hundred feet or more in the air, and then mark his arrow-like flight downward. I have heard this song also in the middle of the night near my cabin. At such times it stands out on the stillness like a bursting rocket on the background of the night.

One or two mornings in April, at a very early hour, I am quite sure to hear the hermit thrush singing in the bushes near my window. How quickly I am transported to the Delectable Mountains and to the mossy solitudes of the northern woods! The winter wren also pauses briefly in his northern journey, and surprises and delights my ear with his sudden lyrical burst of melody. Such a dapper, fidgety, gesticulating, bobbing-up-and-down-and-out-and-in little bird, and yet full of such sweet, wild melody! To get him at his best, one needs to hear him in a dim, northern hemlock wood, where his voice reverberates as in a great hall; just as one should hear the veery in a beech and birch wood, beside a purling trout brook, when the evening shades are falling. It then becomes to you the voice of some particular spirit of the place and the hour. The veery does not inhabit the woods immediately about my cabin, but in the summer twilight he frequently comes up from the valley below and sings along the borders of my territory. How welcome his simple flute-like strain! The wood thrush is the leading chorister in the woods about me. He does not voice the wildness, but seems to give a touch of something half rural, half urban, — such is the power of association in bird-songs. In the evening twilight I often sit on the highest point of the rocky rim of the great granite bowl that holds my three acres of prairie soil, and see the shadows deepen, and listen to the bird voices that rise up from the forest below me. The songs of many wood thrushes make a sort of golden warp in the texture of sounds that is being woven about me. Now the flight-song of the oven-bird holds the ear, then the fainter one of the worm-eating warbler lures it. The carol of the robin, the vesper hymn of the tanager, the flute of the veery, are all on the air. Finally, as

144

the shadows deepen and the stars begin to come out, the whip-poor-will suddenly strikes up. What a rude intrusion upon the serenity and harmony of the hour! A cry without music, insistent, reiterated, loud, penetrating, and yet the ear welcomes it also; the night and the solitude are so vast that they can stand it; and when, an hour later, as the night enters into full possession, the bird comes and serenades me under my window or upon my doorstep, my heart warms toward it. Its cry is a love-call, and there is something of the ardor and persistence of love in it, and when the female responds, and comes and hovers near, there is an interchange of subdued, caressing tones between the two birds that it is a delight to hear. During my first summer here one bird used to strike up every night from a high ledge of rocks in front of my door. At just such a moment in the twilight he would begin, the first to break the stillness. Then the others would follow, till the solitude was vocal with their calls. They are rarely heard later than ten o'clock. Then at daybreak they take up the tale again, whipping poor Will till one pities him. One April morning between three and four o'clock, hearing one strike up near my window, I began counting its calls. My neighbor had told me he had heard one call over two hundred times without a break, which seemed to me a big story. But I have a much bigger one to tell. This bird actually laid upon the back of poor Will

145

one thousand and eighty-eight blows, with only a barely perceptible pause here and there, as if to catch its breath. Then it stopped about half a minute and began again, uttering this time three hundred and ninety calls, when it paused, flew a little farther away, took up the tale once more, and continued till I fell asleep.

By day the whip-poor-will apparently sits motionless upon the ground. A few times in my walks through the woods I have started one up from almost under my feet. On such occasions the bird's movements suggest those of a bat; its wings make no noise, and it wavers about in an uncertain manner, and quickly drops to the ground again. One June day we flushed an old one with her two young, but there was no indecision or hesitation in the manner of the mother bird this time. The young were more than half fledged, and they scampered away a few yards and suddenly squatted upon the ground, where their protective coloring rendered them almost invisible. Then the anxious parent put forth all her arts to absorb our attention and lure us away from her offspring. She flitted before us from side to side, with spread wings and tail, now falling upon the ground, where she would remain a moment as if quite disabled, then perching upon an old stump or low branch with drooping, quivering wings, and imploring us by every gesture to take her and spare her young. My companion had his camera

146

with him, but the bird would not remain long enough in one position for him to get her picture. The whip-poor-will builds no nest, but lays her two blunt, speckled eggs upon the dry leaves, where the plumage of the sitting bird blends perfectly with her surroundings. The eye, only a few feet away, has to search long and carefully to make her out. Every gray and brown and black tint of dry leaf and lichen, and bit of bark or broken twig, is copied in her plumage. In a day or two, after the young are hatched, the mother begins to move about with them through the woods.

When I want the wild of a little different flavor and quality from that immediately about my cabin, I go a mile through the woods to Black Creek, here called the Shattega, and put my canoe into a long, smooth, silent stretch of water that winds through a heavily timbered marsh till it leads into Black Pond, an oval sheet of water half a mile or more across. Here I get the moist, spongy, tranquil, luxurious side of Nature. Here she stands or sits knee-deep in water, and wreathes herself with pond-lilies in summer, and bedecks herself with scarlet maples in autumn. She is an Indian maiden, dark, subtle, dreaming, with glances now and then that thrill the wild blood in one's veins. The Shattega here is a stream without banks and with a just perceptible current. It is a waterway through a timbered marsh. The level floor of the woods ends in an irregular line

147

where the level surface of the water begins. As one glides along in his boat, he sees various rank aquatic growths slowly waving in the shadowy depths beneath him. The larger trees on each side unite their branches above his head, so that at times he seems to be entering an arboreal cave out of which glides the stream. In the more open places the woods mirror themselves in the glassy surface till one seems floating between two worlds, clouds and sky and trees below him matching those around and above him. A bird flits from shore to shore, and one sees it duplicated against the sky in the under-world. What vistas open! What banks of drooping foliage, what grain and arch of gnarled branches, lure the eye as one drifts or silently paddles along! The stream has absorbed the shadows so long that it is itself like a liquid shadow. Its bed is lined with various dark vegetable growths, as with the skin of some huge, shaggy animal, the fur of which slowly stirs in the languid current. I go here in early spring, after the ice has broken up, to get a glimpse of the first wild ducks and to play the sportsman without a gun. I am sure I would not exchange the quiet surprise and pleasure I feel, as, on rounding some point or curve in the stream, two or more ducks spring suddenly out from some little cove or indentation in the shore, and with an alarum *quack*, *quack*, launch into the air and quickly gain the free spaces above the treetops, for the satisfaction of the gunner who sees their dead bodies fall before his murderous fire. He has only a dead duck, which, the chances are, he will not find very toothsome at this season, while I have a live duck with whistling wings cleaving the air northward, where, in some lake or river of Maine or Canada, in late summer, I may meet him again with his brood. It is so easy, too, to bag the game with your eye, while your gun may leave you only a feather or two floating upon the water. The duck has wit, and its wit is as quick as, or quicker than, the sportsman's gun. One day in spring I saw a gunner cut down a duck when it had gained an altitude of thirty or forty feet above the stream. At the report it stopped suddenly, turned a somersault, and fell with a splash into the water. It fell like a brick, and disappeared like one; only a feather and a few bubbles marked the spot where it struck. Had it sunk? No; it had dived. It was probably winged, and in the moment it occupied in falling to the water it had decided what to do. It would go beneath the hunter, since it could not escape above him; it could fly in the water with only one wing, with its feet to aid it. The gunner instantly set up a diligent search in all directions, up and down along the shores, peering long and intently into the depths, thrusting his oar into the weeds and driftwood at the edge of the water, but no duck or sign of duck could he find. It was as if the wounded bird had taken to the mimic heaven that looked so sunny and real down there, and gone on to Canada by that route. What astonished me was that the duck should have kept its presence of mind under such trying circumstances, and not have lost a fraction of a second of time in deciding on a course of action. The duck, I am convinced, has more sagacity than any other of our commoner fowl.

The day I see the first ducks I am pretty sure to come upon the first flock of blackbirds, — rusty grackles, — resting awhile on their northward journey amid the reeds, alders, and spice-bush beside the stream. They allow me to approach till I can see their yellow eyes and the brilliant iris on the necks and heads of the males. Many of them are vocal, and their united voices make a volume of sound that is analogous to a bundle of slivers. Sputtering, splintering, rasping, rending, their notes chafe and excite the ear. They suggest thorns and briers of sound, and yet are most welcome. What voice that rises from our woods or beside our waters in April is not tempered or attuned to the ear? Just as I like to chew the crinkleroot and the twigs of the spice-bush at this time, or at any time, for that matter, so I like to treat my ear to these more aspirated and astringent bird voices. Is it Thoreau who says they are like pepper and salt to this sense? In all the blackbirds we hear the voice of April not yet quite articulate; there is a suggestion of catarrh and influenza still in the air-passages. I should, perhaps, except the red-shouldered starling, whose clear and liquid *gur-ga-lee* or *o-ka-lee*, above the full water-courses, makes a different impression. The cowbird also has a clear note, but it seems to be wrenched or pumped up with much effort.

In May I go to Black Creek to hear the warblers and the water-thrushes. It is the only locality where I have ever heard the two water-thrushes, or accentors, singing at the same time,—the New York and the large-billed. The latter is much more abundant and much the finer songster. How he does make these watery solitudes ring with his sudden, brilliant burst of song! But the more northern species pleases the ear also with his quieter and less hurried strain. I drift in my boat and let the ear attend to the one, then to the other, while the eye takes note of their quick, nervous movements and darting flight. The smaller species probably does not nest along this stream, but the large-billed breeds here abundantly. The last nest I found was in the roots of an up-turned tree, with the water immediately beneath it. I had asked a neighboring farm-boy if he knew of any birds' nests.

"Yes," he said ; and he named over the nests of robins, highholes, sparrows, and others, and then that of a "tip-up."

At this last I pricked up my ears, so to speak. I had not seen a tip-up's nest in many a day. "Where ?" I inquired.

151

"In the roots of a tree in the woods," said Charley.

"Not the nest of the 'tip-up,' or sandpiper," said I. "It builds on the ground in the open country near streams."

"Anyhow, it tipped," replied the boy.

He directed me to the spot, and I found, as I expected to find, the nest of the water-thrush. When the Vassar girls came again, I conducted them to the spot, and they took turns in walking a small tree trunk above the water, and gazing upon a nest brimming with the downy backs of young birds.

When I am listening to the water-thrushes, I am also noting with both eye and ear the warblers and vireos. There comes a week in May when the speckled Canada warblers are in the ascendant. They feed in the low bushes near the water's edge, and are very brisk and animated in voice and movement. The eye easily notes their slate-blue backs and yellow breasts with their broad band of black spots, and the ear quickly discriminates their not less marked and emphatic song.

In late summer I go to the Shattega, and to the lake out of which it flows, for white pond-lilies, and to feast my eye on the masses of purple loosestrife and the more brilliant but more hidden and retired cardinal-flower that bloom upon its banks. One cannot praise the pond-lily; his best words mar it, like the insects that eat its petals: but he can contemplate it as it opens in the morning sun and distills such perfume, such purity, such snow of petal and such gold of anther, from the dark water and still darker ooze. How feminine it seems beside its coarser and more robust congeners ; how shy, how pliant, how fine in texture and star-like in form!

The loosestrife is a foreign plant, but it has made itself thoroughly at home here, and its masses of royal purple make the woods look civil and festive. The cardinal burns with a more intense fire, and fairly lights up the little dark nooks where it glasses itself in the still water. One must pause and look at it. Its intensity, its pure scarlet, the dark background upon which it is projected, its image in the still darker water, and its general air of retirement and seclusion, all arrest and delight the eye. It is a heart-throb of color on the bosom of the dark solitude.

The rarest and wildest animal that my neighborhood boasts of is the otter. Every winter we see the tracks of one or more of them upon the snow along Black Creek. But the eye that has seen the animal itself in recent years I cannot find. It probably makes its excursions along the creek by night. Follow its track — as large as that of a fair-sized dog — over the ice, and you will find that it ends at every open pool and rapid, and begins again upon the ice beyond. Sometimes it makes little excursions up the bank, its body often dragging in the snow like a log. My son followed the track one day far up the mountain-side, where the absence of the snow caused him to lose it. I like to think of so wild and shy a creature holding its own within sound of the locomotive's whistle.

The fox passes my door in winter, and probably in summer too, as do also the 'possum and the coon. The latter tears down my sweet corn in the garden, and the rabbit eats off my raspberry-bushes and nibbles my first strawberries, while the woodchucks eat my celery and beans and peas. Chipmunks carry off the corn I put out for the chickens, and weasels eat the chickens themselves.

Many times during the season I have in my solitude a visit from a bald eagle. There is a dead tree near the summit, where he often perches, and which we call the "old eagle-tree." It is a pine, killed years ago by a thunderbolt, — the bolt of Jove, — and now the bird of Jove hovers about it or sits upon it. I have little doubt that what attracted me to this spot attracts him, — the seclusion, the savageness, the elemental grandeur. Sometimes, as I look out of my window early in the morning, I see the eagle upon his perch, preening his plumage, or waiting for the rising sun to gild the mountain-tops. When the smoke begins to rise from my chimney, or he sees me going to the spring for water, he concludes it is time for him to be off. But he need not fear the crack of the rifle here; nothing more deadly than field-glasses shall be pointed at him while I am about. Often in the course of the day I see him circling above my domain, or winging his way toward the mountains. His home is apparently in the Shawangunk Range, twenty or more miles distant, and I fancy he stops or lingers above me on his way to the river. The days on which I see him are not quite the same as the other days. I think my thoughts soar a little higher all the rest of the morning: I have had a visit from a messenger of Jove. The lift or range of those great wings has passed into my thought. I once heard a collector get up in a scientific body and tell how many eggs of the bald eagle he had clutched that season, how many from this nest, how many from that, and how one of the eagles had deported itself after he had killed its mate. I felt ashamed for him. He had only proved himself a superior human weasel. The man with the rifle and the man with the collector's craze are fast reducing the number of eagles in the country. Twenty years ago I used to see a dozen or more along the river in the spring when the ice was breaking up, where I now see only one or two, or none at all. In the present case, what would it profit me could I find and plunder my eagle's nest, or strip his skin from his dead carcass? Should I know him better? I do not want to know him that way. I want rather to feel the inspiration of his presence and noble bearing. I want my interest and sympathy to go with him in his continental voyaging

155

up and down, and in his long, elevated flights to and from his eyrie upon the remote, solitary cliffs. He draws great lines across the sky ; he sees the forests like a carpet beneath him, he sees the hills and valleys as folds and wrinkles in a many-colored tapestry ; he sees the river as a silver belt connecting remote horizons. We climb mountain-peaks to get a glimpse of the spectacle that is hourly spread out beneath him. Dignity, elevation, repose, are his. I would have my thoughts take as wide a sweep. I would be as far removed from the petty cares and turmoils of this noisy and blustering world.

III

NEW GLEANINGS IN OLD FIELDS

ONE of the good signs of the times is the interest our young people are taking in the birds, and the numerous clubs and societies that are being formed throughout the country for bird protection and bird study. In my youth but little was heard about the birds. They were looked upon as of small account. Many of them were treated as the farmer's natural enemies. Crows and all kinds of hawks and owls were destroyed whenever chance offered. I knew a farmer who every summer caught and killed all the red-tailed hawks he could. He stood up poles in his meadows, upon the tops of which he would set steel traps. The hawks, looking for meadow-mice, would alight upon them and be caught. The farmer was thus slaying some of his best friends, as these large hawks live almost entirely upon mice and other vermin. The redtail, or hen-hawk, is very wary of a man with a gun, but he has not yet learned of the danger that lurks in a steel trap on the top of a pole.

If a strict account could be kept with our crows

and hawks for a year, it would be found at the end
of that time that most of them had a balance to their
credit. They do us more good than injury. A few
of them, such as the fish crow, the sharp-shinned
hawk, Cooper's hawk, and the duck hawk, are destructive to song-birds and wild fowl; but the others
subsist mainly upon insects and vermin.

One August, when I was a boy, I remember a
great flight of sparrow hawks, — so called, I suppose, because they rarely if ever catch sparrows.
They were seen by the dozen, hovering above and
flitting about the meadows. On carefully observing
them, I found they were catching grasshoppers, —
the large, fat ones found in the meadows in late
summer. They would poise on the wing twenty
or thirty feet above the ground, after the manner
of the larger hawks watching for mice, then suddenly drop down and seize their prey, which they
devoured on the limb of a tree or a stake in the fence.
They lingered about for several days and then drifted
away.

Nearly every season a pair of broad-winged
hawks — about a size smaller than the hen-hawk —
build their nest in the woods not far from my cabin.
You may know this hawk by its shrill, piercing cry,
the smoothest, most ear-piercing note I know of
in the woods. They utter this cry when you approach
their nest, and continue to utter it as long as you
linger about. One season they built in a large pine-

158

tree near which I frequently passed in my walk. Always, as I came near, I would hear this wild, shrill plaint, made, I think, by the mother bird. Often she would sit upon a branch in full view and utter her ear-dividing protest. There were never any signs about the nest that birds or poultry formed part of the food of the young. It is said that this hawk subsists principally upon insects and frogs. When the young — two of them — were about two thirds grown, they used to perch upon the edge of the nest and upon one of the branches that held it in place.

One day I took a couple of bird enthusiasts there to hear the cry of the mother hawk. We lingered about for nearly an hour, and not a sound was heard nor a parent hawk seen. Then I tried to stir up the young, but without effect. They regarded us intently, but made no move and uttered no cry. A smaller tree grew beside the pine that held the nest. Up this I climbed till within probably twenty-five feet of the suspicious young; then I reached out my foot and planted it upon a limb of the larger tree. Instantly, as if the tree were a vital part of themselves, the young hawks took the alarm and launched into the air. But the wings of one of them could not long sustain him, and he came to the ground within twenty yards of the foot of the tree. As we approached him his attitude of defense was striking, — wings half spread, beak open, one foot raised, and a look of defiance in his eye. But we soon reassured him, and presently left him perched upon a branch in a much more composed state of mind. The parent hawks did not appear upon the scene during our stay.

II

I do not share the alarm expressed in some quarters over the seeming decrease in the numbers of our birds. We are always more or less pessimistic in regard to the present time and present things. As we grow older, the number of beautiful things in the world seems to diminish. The Indian summer is not what it used to be; the winters are not so bracing; the spring is more uncertain; and honest men are fewer. But there is not much change, after all. The change is mainly in us. I find no decrease in the great body of our common field, orchard, and wood birds, though I do not see the cliff swallows I used to see in my youth; they go farther north, to northern New England and Canada. Our smart new farm buildings with their dressed and painted clapboards do not attract them. At Rangeley Lake, in Maine, I saw the eaves of barns as crowded with their mud nests as I used to see the eaves of my father's barns amid the Catskills. In the cliffs along the Yukon in Alaska they are said to swarm in great numbers. The cliffs along the upper Columbia show thousands of their nests. Nearly all our game-birds are decreasing in numbers, because sportsmen are more and more numerous and skillful, and their guns more and more deadly. The bobolinks are fewer than they were a decade or two ago, because they are slaughtered more and more in the marshes and rice-fields of the South. The bluebirds and hermit thrushes were threatened with extinction by a cold wave and a severe storm in the Southern States, a few years ago. These birds appear to have perished by the hundred thousand. But they have slowly recovered lost ground, and seem now to be as numerous as ever. I see fewer eagles along the Hudson River than I used to see fifteen years ago. The collectors and the riflemen are no doubt responsible for this decrease. But the robins, thrushes, finches, warblers, black-birds, orioles, flycatchers, vireos, and woodpeckers are quite as abundant as they were a quarter of a century ago, if not more so.

The English sparrows, no doubt, tend to run out our native birds in towns and smaller cities, but in the country this effect is not noticeable. They are town birds anyhow, and naturally take their place with a thousand other town abominations. A friend of mine who lives in the heart of a city of twenty thousand people amused me by recounting his obser-vation upon a downy woodpecker that had made up its mind to pass the winter in town. In November it began to excavate a chamber for its winter quarters in the dead branch of a maple that stood on the curb in front of my friend's window. The English sparrows sat about upon the branches, regarding the proceeding with evident interest, but showing no inclination to interfere. "Let him work," they seemed to say; "something interesting may come of it." For two weeks or more Downy was busy carving out his retreat. At last it was finished ; but when he returned one night he found it occupied, and the occupant refused to vacate it. This seemed to puzzle the woodpecker a good deal. Every night he was barred out of his own house. Then he took it into his head to come home earlier in the day. This scheme worked at first, but soon the sparrows clubbed together, assaulted his castle, and literally dragged him out by sheer force. Then he gave up the fight, and no doubt returned to the country a sadder and a wiser bird. A new retreat had to be drilled out; an undertaking which must have caused him no little solicitude. It would be interesting to know where, in the mean time, he passed the night. Probably in some old retreat of his or his friends'.

How to get rid of the English sparrows, or to keep them in check, is a question that is agitating many of our communities. A sporadic effort here and there will not have much effect; there must be concerted action over a wide area. The blow must be struck in their breeding-haunts. In every town that has a police force, let it be one of the duties of the police to spy out their nesting-places and report to headquarters, as they would any other nuisance or misdemeanor. Then let men be detailed to break them up. As long as the nest is untouched, killing the birds is of little avail. A friend of mine, a well-known ornithologist, told me that one summer he and his wife took for the season a house in a small town not far from Boston. There were two sparrows' nests in the cavities of two fruit trees in the garden. At once he opened war upon the parent birds. He shot one of them. In two hours the male or female, whichever it was, had another mate. He continued the shooting. Whenever a bird showed itself about either nest it was shot. In consequence the birds became very wild and shrewd, till he was compelled to fire from a crack in the door. But he kept up the warfare till he had killed sixty-two birds about those nests, and yet from each cavity a brood of young birds came forth. I suppose there were eggs or young in the nest when my friend appeared upon the scene, and that he did not in any one day kill both the parent birds. Had he done so, it is still a question whether the young would have been allowed to perish. Their cries would probably have attracted other birds.

The parental instinct is strong in most creatures. Birds as well as animals will sometimes adopt the young of others. I have been told of a bluebird that took it upon himself to help feed some young vireos in a nest near his own, and of a house wren that carried food to some young robins.

Last summer I witnessed a similar occurrence, and made this record in my note-book: "A nest of young robins in the maple in front of the house being fed by a chipping sparrow. The little sparrow is very attentive; seems decidedly fond of her adopted babies. The old robins resent her services, and hustle her out of the tree whenever they find her near the nest. (It was this hurried departure of Chippy from the tree that first attracted my attention.) She watches her chances, and comes with food in their absence. The young birds are about ready to fly, and when the chippy feeds them her head fairly disappears in their capacious mouths. She jerks it back as if she were afraid of being swallowed. Then she lingers near them on the edge of the nest, and seems to admire them. When she sees the old robin coming, she spreads her wings in an attitude of defense, and then flies away. I wonder if she has had the experience of rearing a cow-bunting?" (A day later.) "The robins are out of the nest, and the little sparrow continues to feed them. She approaches them rather timidly and hesitatingly, as if she feared they might swallow her, then thrusts her titbit quickly into the distended mouth and jerks back."

Whether the chippy had lost her own brood, whether she was an unmated bird, or whether the case was simply the overflowing of the maternal instinct, it would be interesting to know.

III

I am glad to see that this growing interest in bird life has reached our schools and is being promoted there. I often receive letters from teachers touching these matters. A teacher in the State of Delaware wrote me that he and his pupils were trying to know all the birds within a mile of their schoolhouse. One species of bird had puzzled them much. The teacher frequently saw the birds feeding in the road in the evening as he walked home from school. Then, when the blizzard came, they approached the school-house for crumbs, sometimes in loose flocks of a dozen or more.

This is the teacher's description of the bird: —

"The upper half of its bill is dark, and about one third on the tips of the lower. The rest is light. The feathers are a greenish yellow below the bill, and the throat feathers are black with white tips. The belly is white, but the feathers are black underneath. In size it is a little smaller than the robin. It has a chirp, when flying, something like the cedar-bird. The back toe is certainly very long for so small a bird."

Had not this description been accompanied by a wing, leg, and tail of the bird in question, I should have been at a loss to name it. One of the birds was found dead in the snow beneath the telegraph wires, and this afforded the samples. It proved to be the prairie horned lark, one of our migrants, which passes

165

the winter near the snow-line in the Southern States, and the summer in the hilly parts of New York, New England, and Canada.

The above description makes the bird much too large, as its size is nearer that of the bobolink and the bluebird. All the larks have the hind toe very prominent. This species, like the true skylark, is entirely a terrestrial bird, and never alights upon trees. When singing it soars and hovers high in air like the skylark, but its song is a very crude, feeble affair in comparison with that of the latter. Its winter plumage is far less marked than its summer dress. One day I took note of one singing above my native hills, when it repeated its feeble, lisping song one hundred and three times before it closed its wings and dropped to the earth precisely as does the European skylark.

Another teacher writes me asking if the blue jay eats acorns. She is sure she has seen them flying away from oak-trees with acorns in their beaks, and yet some authority to whom she had appealed was doubtful about their eating them. It is quite certain that jays eat acorns, but they carry away and hide a great many more than they eat. The thieving propensity of the jay, which is a trait of his family, the *Corvidæ*, leads him to carry away chestnuts and acorns and hide them in the grass and under leaves, and thus makes him an unsuspecting instrument in the planting of forests. This is the reason why, when a pine or hemlock forest is cut away, oaks and chestnuts are so likely to spring up. These nuts can be disseminated only by the aid of birds and squirrels.

A clergyman writes me from a New England town of something he found in his winter walks that puzzled him very much. It was an old cocoon of the cecropia moth, in which he found two kernels of corn. What creature could have put them there, and for what purpose? Of course it was the blue jay; he had hidden the corn in the same blind way that he hides the acorns. I have seen jays in winter carry away corn and put it into an old worm's nest in a wild-cherry tree, and drop it into knot-holes in the tree trunk. It is doubtful if the jay can digest corn swallowed whole. It is too hard a grist for his mill. He will peck out the chit or softer germinal part, as will the chickadee, and devour that.

Another teacher wrote me that two pretty birds, strangers to her, had built their nest in a pear-tree near the kitchen door of her house.

They were small and slender, the male of a ruddy brown, his head, tail, and wings black, and the female yellowish green, with darker wings. The male brought worms and fed his mate while she was sitting, and seemed the happiest bird alive, save when the kittens romped about the door; and then, even in the midst of his cries of alarm like a blackbird's, he would burst out with glad notes of rejoicing, a song to her ear like a sparrow's. Soon there were young in the nest, and the air was filled with the constant fluttering of wings and the rapturous song of the father. But alas! one morning found the nest rifled of its treasures, and only the silent, miserable male flitting in and about the home in the most heartbroken fashion. A red squirrel or a cat or an owl had done the mischief. The nest was woven of hemp and grasses, and was suspended from the fork of a limb. The teacher guessed rightly that the bird was a near relative of the Baltimore oriole; it was the orchard oriole, a much rarer bird and a much finer songster. The song is not like a sparrow's, but much louder, stronger, and more ecstatic. The male does not get his full uniform of black and bay till the fourth summer.

A college boy once wrote me that he had seen a mother oriole fall down dead when her nest was being robbed. The nest was in a large sycamore about twenty-five feet from the ground. An old Frenchman living near wanted one of the eggs for his collection. He procured a long pole, armed with some sharp nails on the end, and from the top of a small building under the tree tried to cut off the nest from the branch. The mother bird kept her place within till it began to yield before the assault. Instead of eggs, the nest held young birds. When one of them fell out, the mother bird flew down and screamed around it in great excitement. Before the man could loosen his pole from the nest, all the young birds had fallen to the ground. The mother was darting and screaming about them, when suddenly she fell to the ground dead, a victim, no doubt, to her excessive emotion of grief. Birds are very delicate, high-strung creatures, and probably die of apoplexy or heart failure as frequently as human beings.

IV

Love the wood-rose, but leave it on its stalk, hints the poet. So, I say, find a bird's nest, but touch not the eggs. It seems to profane the nest even to touch its contents with the utmost care. One June day, I found the nest of the yellow-winged sparrow, — the sparrow one often hears in our fields and meadows, that has a song that suggests a grasshopper. I was sitting on the fence that bounded a hill meadow, watching the horned larks, and hoping that one of them would disclose the locality of its nest. A few yards from me was a small bush, from the top of which a yellow-winged sparrow was sending out its feeble, stridulous song. Presently a little brown bird came out of the meadow and alighted in the grass but a few yards from the singer. Instantly he flew to the spot, and I knew it was his mate. They seemed to have some conversation together there in the grass, when, in a moment or two, they separated, the male flitting to his perch on the bush and continuing his song, while the female disappeared quickly into the grass ten or more yards away. "The nest is there," I said, "and I must find it." So I walked straight to the spot where the bird had vanished and scrutinized the ground closely. Not seeing the object of my search, I dropped my handkerchief upon the grass, and began walking cautiously about it in circles, covering more and more ground, and scanning closely every foot of the meadow-bottom. Suddenly, when I was four or five yards from my handkerchief, a little dark-brown bird fluttered out almost from under my feet, and the pretty secret was mine.

The nest, made of dry grass and a few hairs, was sunk into the ground, — into the great, brownish-gray, undistinguished meadow surface, — and held four speckled eggs. The mother bird fluttered through the grass, and tried, by feigning disablement, to lure me away from the spot. I had noticed that the male had ceased singing as soon as I began my search, and had showed much uneasiness. He now joined the female, and two more agitated birds I had never seen. The actions of this bird are quick and nervous at all times ; now they became almost frenzied. But I quickly withdrew, and concealed myself behind the fence. After a brief consultation the birds withdrew also, and it was nearly a half-hour before they returned. Then the mother bird, after much feigning and flitting nervously about, dropped into the grass several yards

170

from the nest. I fancied her approaching it in a cautious, circuitous, indirect way.

In the afternoon I came again; also the next day; but at no time did I find the male in song on his old perch. He seemed to take the blame of the accident upon himself; he had betrayed the locality of the nest; and now I found him upon the fence or upon an apple-tree far off, where his presence or his song would not give away the precious secret.

The male bird of almost every species is careful about being much in evidence very near the nest. You will generally find him in song along the rim of a large circle of which the nest is the centre. I have known poets to represent the bird singing upon its nest, but if this ever happens, it is a very rare occurrence.

IV

BIRD LIFE IN WINTER

THE distribution of our birds over the country in summer is like that of the people, quite uniform. Every wood and field has its quota, and no place so barren but it has some bird to visit it. One knows where to look for sparrows and thrushes and bobolinks and warblers and flycatchers. But the occupation of the country by our winter residents is like the Indian occupation of the land. They are found in little bands, a few here and there, with large tracts quite untenanted.

One may walk for hours through the winter woods and not see or hear a bird. Then he may come upon a troop of chickadees, with a nuthatch or two in their wake, and maybe a downy woodpecker. Birds not of a feather flock together at this inclement season. The question of food is always an urgent one. Evidently the nuthatch thinks there must be food where the chickadees flit and call so cheerily, and the woodpecker is probably drawn to the nuthatch for a similar reason.

Together they make a pretty thorough search, — fine, finer, finest. The chickadee explores the twigs and smaller branches; what he gets is on the surface, and so fine as to be almost microscopic. The nuthatch explores the trunks and larger branches of the trees; he goes a little deeper, into crevices of the bark and under lichens. Then comes Downy, who goes deeper still. He bores for larger game through the bark, and into the trunks and branches themselves.

In late fall this band is often joined by the golden-crowned kinglet and the brown creeper. The kinglet is finer-eyed and finer-billed than even the chickadee, and no doubt gathers what the latter overlooks, while the brown creeper, with his long, slender, curved bill, takes what both the nuthatch and the woodpecker miss. Working together, it seems as if they must make a pretty clean sweep. But the trees are numerous and large, and the birds are few. Only a mere fraction of tree surface is searched over at any one time. In large forests probably only a mere fraction of the trees are visited at all.

One cold day in midwinter, when I was walking through the snowless woods, I saw chickadees, nuthatches, and woodpeckers upon the ground, and upon roots and fallen branches. They were looking for the game that had fallen, as a boy looks for apples under the tree.

The winter wren is so called because he sometimes braves our northern winters, but it is rarely that one sees him at this season. I think I have seen him only two or three times in winter in my life. The event of one long walk, recently, in February, was seeing one of these birds. As I followed a byroad, beside a little creek in the edge of a wood, my eye caught a glimpse of a small brown bird darting under a stone bridge. I thought to myself no bird but a wren would take refuge under so small a bridge as that. I stepped down upon it and expected to see the bird dart out at the upper end. As it did not appear, I scrutinized the bank of the little run, covered with logs and brush, a few rods farther up.

Presently I saw the wren curtsying and gesticulating beneath an old log. As I approached he disappeared beneath some loose stones in the bank, then came out again and took another peep at me, then fidgeted about for a moment and disappeared again, running in and out of the holes and recesses and beneath the rubbish like a mouse or a chipmunk. The winter wren may always be known by these squatting, bobbing-out-and-in habits.

As I sought a still closer view of him, he flitted stealthily a few yards up the run and disappeared beneath a small plank bridge near a house.

I wondered what he could feed upon at such a time. There was a light skim of snow upon the ground, and the weather was cold. The wren, so far as I know, is entirely an insect-feeder, and where can he find insects in midwinter in our climate ? Probably by searching under bridges, under brush heaps, in holes and cavities in banks where the sun falls warm.

175

In such places he may find dormant spiders and flies and other hibernating insects or their larvæ. We have a tiny, mosquito-like creature that comes forth in March or in midwinter, as soon as the temperature is a little above freezing. One may see them performing their fantastic air-dances when the air is so chilly that one buttons his overcoat about him in his walk. They are darker than the mosquito, — a sort of dark water-color, — and are very frail to the touch. Maybe the wren knows the hiding-place of these insects.

With food in abundance, no doubt many more of our birds would brave the rigors of our winters. I have known a pair of bluebirds to brave them on such poor rations as are afforded by the hardhack or sugarberry, — a drupe the size of a small pea, with a thin, sweet skin. Probably hardly one per cent. of the drupe is digestible food. Bluebirds in December will also eat the berries of the poison ivy, as will the downy woodpecker.

Robins will pass the winter with us when the cover of a pine or hemlock forest can be had near a supply of red cedar berries. The cedar-bird probably finds little other food in the valley of the Hudson and in New England, yet I see occasional flocks of them every winter month.

Sometimes the chickadees and nuthatches, hunting through the winter woods, make a discovery that brings every bird within hearing to the spot, — they spy out the screech owl hiding in the thick of a hem-lock-tree. What an event it is in the day's experience! It sets the whole clan agog.

While I was walking in the December woods, one day, my attention was attracted by a great hue and cry among these birds. I found them in and about a hemlock-tree, — eight or ten chickadees and four or five red-bellied nuthatches. Such a chiding chorus of tiny voices I had not heard for a long time. The tone was not that of alarm so much as it was that of trouble and displeasure.

I gazed long and long up into the dark, dense green mass of the tree to make out the cause of all this excitement. The chickadees were clinging to the ends of the sprays, as usual, apparently very busy looking for food, and all the time uttering their shrill plaint. The nuthatches perched about upon the branches or ran up and down the tree trunks, inces-santly piping their displeasure. At last I made out the cause of the disturbance, — a little owl on a limb, looking down in wide-eyed intentness upon me. How annoyed he must have felt at all this hullabaloo, this lover of privacy and quiet, to have his name cried from the treetops, and his retreat advertised to every passer-by!

I have never known woodpeckers to show any excitement at the presence of hawk or owl, probably because they are rarely preyed upon by these ma-rauders. In their nests and in their winter quarters,

deeply excavated in trunk or branch of tree, woodpeckers are beyond the reach of both beak and claw.

The day I saw the winter wren I saw two golden-
crowned kinglets fly from one sycamore to another
in an open field, uttering their fine call-notes. That
so small a body can brave the giant cold of our winters seems remarkable enough. These are mainly
birds of the evergreens, although at times they frequent the groves and the orchards.

How does the ruby-crowned kinglet know he has
a brilliant bit of color on his crown which he can
uncover at will, and that this has great charms for
the female? During the rivalries of the males in
the mating season, and in the autumn also, they
flash this brilliant ruby at each other. I witnessed
what seemed to be a competitive display of this
kind one evening in November. I was walking along
the road, when my ear was attracted by the fine,
shrill lisping and piping of a small band of these
birds in an apple-tree. I paused to see what was the
occasion of so much noise and bluster among these
tiny bodies. There were four or five of them, all
more or less excited, and two of them especially so.
I think the excitement of the others was only a
reflection of that of these two. These were hopping
around each other, apparently peering down upon
something beneath them. I suspected a cat concealed behind the wall, and so looked over, but
there was nothing there. Observing them more

closely, I saw that the two birds were entirely occupied with each other.

They behaved exactly as if they were comparing crowns, and each extolling his own. Their heads were bent forward, the red crown patch uncovered and showing as a large, brilliant cap, their tails were spread, and the side feathers below the wings were fluffed out. They did not come to blows, but followed each other about amid the branches, uttering their thin, shrill notes and displaying their ruby crowns to the utmost. Evidently it was some sort of strife or dispute or rivalry that centred about this brilliant patch.

Few persons seem aware that the goldfinch is also a winter bird, — it is so brilliant and familiar in summer and so neutral and withdrawn in winter. The call-note and manner of flight do not change, but the color of the males and their habits are very different from their color and habits in summer. In winter they congregate in small, loose flocks, both sexes of a dusky yellowish brown, and feed upon the seeds of grasses and weeds that stand above the snow in fields and along fences.

Day after day I have observed a band of five or six of them feeding amid the dry stalks of the evening primrose by the roadside. They are adepts in extracting the seed from the pods. How pretty their call to each other at such times, — *paisley* or *peasely*, with the rising inflection!

The only one of our winter birds that really seems a part of the winter, that seems to be born of the whirling snow, and to be happiest when storms drive thickest and coldest, is the snow bunting, the real snowbird, with plumage copied from the fields where the drifts hide all but the tops of the tallest weeds, — large spaces of pure white touched here and there with black and gray and brown. Its twittering call and chirrup coming out of the white obscurity is the sweetest and happiest of all winter bird sounds. It is like the laughter of children. The fox-hunter hears it on the snowy hills, the farmer hears it when he goes to fodder his cattle from the distant stack, the country schoolboy hears it as he breaks his way through the drifts toward the school. It is ever a voice of good cheer and contentment.

One March, during a deep snow, a large flock of buntings stayed about my vineyards for several days, feeding upon the seeds of redroot and other weeds that stood above the snow. What boyhood associations their soft and cheery calls brought up! How plump and well-fed and hardy they looked, and how alert and suspicious they were! They evidently had had experiences with hawks and shrikes. Every minute or two they would all spring into the air as one bird, circle about for a moment, then alight upon the snow again. Occasionally one would perch upon a wire or grapevine, as if to keep watch and ward

Presently, while I stood in front of my study look

ing at them, a larger and darker bird came swiftly by me, flying low and straight toward the buntings. He shot beneath the trellises, and evidently hoped to surprise the birds. It was a shrike, thirsting for blood or brains. But the buntings were on the alert, and were up in the air before the feathered assassin reached them. As the flock wheeled about, he joined them and flew along with them for some distance, but made no attempt to strike that I could see.

Presently he left them and perched upon the top of a near maple. The birds did not seem to fear him now, but swept past the treetop where he sat as if to challenge him to a race, and then went their way. I have seen it stated that these birds, when suddenly surprised by a hawk, will dive beneath the snow to escape him. They doubtless roost upon the ground, as do most ground-builders, and hence must often be covered by the falling snow.

V

A BIRDS' FREE LUNCH

ONE winter, during four or five weeks of severe weather, several of our winter birds were pensioners upon my bounty, — three blue jays, two downy woodpeckers, three chickadees, and one kinglet, — and later a snowbird — junco — appeared.

I fastened pieces of suet and marrow-bones upon the tree in front of my window, then, as I sat at my desk, watched the birds at their free lunch. The jays bossed the woodpeckers, the woodpeckers bossed the chickadees, and the chickadees bossed the kinglet.

Sometimes in my absence a crow would swoop down and boss the whole crew and carry off the meat. The kinglet was the least of all, — a sort of "hop-o'-my-thumb" bird. He became quite tame, and one day alighted upon my arm as I stood leaning against the tree. I could have put my hand upon him several times. I wonder where the midget roosted. He was all alone. He liked the fare so well that he seemed disposed to stop till spring. During one terrible night of wind and snow and zero temperature I feared he would be swept away. I thought of him in the middle of the night, when the violence of the storm kept me from sleep. Imagine this solitary atom in feathers drifting about in the great arctic out-of-doors and managing to survive. I fancied him in one of my thick spruces, his head under his tiny wing, buffeted by wind and snow, his little black feet clinging to the perch, and wishing that morning would come.

The fat meat is fuel for him; it keeps up the supply of animal heat. None of the birds will eat lean meat; they want the clear fat. The jays alight upon it and peck away with great vigor, almost standing on tiptoe to get the proper sweep. The woodpecker uses his head alone in pecking, but the jay's action involves the whole body. Yet his blows are softer, not so sharp and abrupt as those of the woodpecker. Pecking is not exactly his business.

He swallows the morsel eagerly, watching all the time lest some enemy surprise him in the act. Indeed, one noticeable thing about all the birds is their nervousness while eating. The chickadee turns that bead-like eye of his in all directions incessantly, lest something seize him while he is not looking. He is not off his guard for a moment. It is almost painful to observe the state of fear in which he lives. He will not keep his place upon the bone longer than a few seconds at a time lest he become a mark for some enemy,— a hawk, a shrike, or a cat.

184

One would not think the food would digest when taken in such haste and trepidation.

While the jays are feeding, swallowing morsel after morsel very rapidly, the chickadees flit about in an anxious, peevish manner, lest there be none left for themselves.

I suspect the jays carry the food off and hide it, as they certainly do corn when I put it out for the hens. The jay has a capacious throat; he will lodge half a dozen or more kernels of corn in it, stretching his neck up as he takes them, to give them room, and then fly away to an old bird's-nest or a caterpillar's nest and deposit them in it. But in this respect the little kettle cannot call the big pot black. The chickadee also will carry away what it cannot eat. One day I dug a dozen or more white grubs — the larvæ of some beetle — out of a decayed maple on my woodpile and placed them upon my window-sill. The chickadees soon discovered them, and fell to carrying them off as fast as ever they could, distributing them among the branches of the Norway spruces. Among the grubs was one large white one half the size of one's little finger. One of the chickadees seized this; it was all he could carry, but he made off with it. The mate to this grub I found rolled up in a smooth cell in a mass of decayed wood at the heart of the old maple referred to; it was full of frost. I carried it in by the fire, and the next day it was alive and apparently

185

wanted to know what had brought spring so suddenly.

How rapidly birds live! Their demand for food is almost incessant. This colony of mine appear to feed every eight or ten minutes. Their little mills grind their grist very rapidly. Once in my walk upon the sea beach I encountered two small beach birds running up and down in the edge of the surf, keeping just in the thin, lace-like edging of the waves, and feeding upon the white, cricket-like hoppers that quickly buried themselves in the sand as the waters retreated. I kept company with the birds till they ceased to be afraid of me. They would feed eagerly for a few minutes and then stop, stand on one leg and put their heads under their wings for two or three minutes, and then resume their feeding, so rapidly did they digest their food. But all birds digest very rapidly.

My two woodpeckers seldom leave the tree upon which the food is placed. One is a male, as is shown by his red plume, and the other a female. There is not a bit of kindness or amity between them. Indeed, there is open hostility. The male will not allow the female even to look at the meat while he is feeding. She will sidle around toward it, edging nearer and nearer, when he will suddenly dart at her, and often pursue her till she leaves the tree. Every hour in the day I see him trying to drive her from the neighborhood. She stands in perpetual dread of him.

186

and gives way the instant he approaches. He is
a tyrant and a bully. They both pass the night
in snug chambers which they have excavated in
the decayed branch of an old apple-tree, but not
together.

But in the spring what a change will come over
the male. He will protest to the female that he was
only in fun, that she took him far too seriously,
that he had always cherished a liking for her. Last
April I saw a male trying his blandishments upon a
female in this way. It may have been the same pair
I am now observing. The female was extremely shy
and reluctant; evidently she was skeptical of the sin-
cerity of so sudden a change on the part of the male.
I saw him pursue her from tree to tree with the most
flattering attention. The flight of the woodpecker
is at all times undulating, but on such occasions
this feature is so enhanced and the whole action so
affected and studied on the part of the male that
the scene becomes highly amusing. The female flew
down upon a low stump in the currant-patch and was
very busy about her own affairs; the male followed.
alighted on something several rods distant, and appeared to be equally busy about his affairs. Presently
the female made quite a long flight to a tree by the
roadside. I could not tell how the male knew she had
flown and what course she had taken, as he was hidden from her amid the thick currant-bushes; but
he did know, and soon followed after in his curious

exaggerated undulatory manner of flight. I have little doubt that his suit was finally successful.

I watch these woodpeckers daily to see if I can solve the mystery as to how they hop up and down the trunks and branches without falling away from them when they let go their hold. They come down a limb or trunk backward by a series of little hops, moving both feet together. If the limb is at an angle to the tree and they are on the under side of it, they do not fall away from it to get a new hold an inch or half inch farther down. They are held to it as steel to a magnet. Both tail and head are involved in the feat. At the instant of making the hop the head is thrown in and the tail thrown out, but the exact mechanics of it I cannot penetrate. Philosophers do not yet know how a backward-falling cat turns in the air, but turn she does. It may be that the woodpecker never quite relaxes his hold, though to my eye he appears to do so.

Birds nearly always pass the night in such places as they select for their nests, — ground-builders upon the ground, tree-builders upon trees. I have seen an oriole ensconce himself for the night amid the thick cluster of leaves on the end of a maple branch, where soon after his mate built her nest.

My chickadees, true to this rule, pass the arctic winter nights in little cavities in the trunks of trees like the woodpeckers. One cold day, about four o'clock, while it was snowing and blowing, I heard, as I was unharnessing my horse near the old apple-tree, the sharp, chiding note of a chickadee. On looking for the bird I failed to see him. Suspecting the true cause of his sudden disappearance, I took a pole and touched a limb that had an opening in its end where the wrens had the past season had a nest. As I did so, out came the chickadee and scolded sharply. The storm and the cold had driven him early to his chamber. The snow buntings are said to plunge into the snow-banks and pass the night there. We know the ruffed grouse does this.

VI

TWO BIRDS'-NESTS

I CONSIDER myself lucky if, in the course of a season, I can pick up two or three facts in natural history that are new to me. To have a new delight in an old or familiar fact is not always easy, and is perhaps quite as much to be desired. The familiar we always have with us; to see it with fresh eyes so as to find a new pleasure in it, — that is a great point.

I think one never sees a bird's-nest of any kind without fresh pleasure. It is such a charming secret, and is usually so well kept by the tree, or bank, or bit of ground that holds it; and then it is such a dainty and exquisite cradle or nursery amid its rough and wild surroundings, — a point so cherished and cared for in the apparently heedless economy of the fields or woods!

When it is a new nest and one long searched for, the pleasure is of course proportionally greater. Such a pleasure came to me one day last summer in early July, when I discovered the nest of the water-thrush or water-wagtail.

The nest of its cousin the oven-bird, called by the

old ornithologists the golden-crowned thrush, was familiar to me, as it probably is to most country boys, — a nest partly thrust under the dry leaves upon the ground in the woods, and holding four or five whitish eggs covered with reddish-brown spots. The mother bird is in size less than the sparrow, and in color is a light olive with a speckled breast, and she is the prettiest walker to be seen in the woods.

The water-accentor or wagtail is a much rarer bird, and of a darker olive green. As the color of the oven-bird harmonizes with the dry leaves over which it walks, so the color of the wagtail is in keeping with the dark-veined brooks and forest pools along which it flits and near which it nests.

With me it is an April bird. When the spice-bush is in bloom along the fringes of the creeks, and the leaves of the adder's-tongue or fawn lily have pierced the mould, I expect to hear the water-thrush. Its song is abrupt, bright, and ringing. It contrasts with its surroundings as does the flower of the blood-root which you may have seen that day.

It is the large-billed or Louisiana water-thrush of which I am speaking. The other species, the New York water-accentor, is rarer with me, and goes farther into the mountains.

The large-billed is a quick, shy, emphatic bird in its manner. Some birds, such as the true thrushes, impress one as being of a serene, contemplative disposition; there is a kind of harmony and tranquillity in all their movements; but the bird I am speaking of is sharp, restless, hurried. Its song is brilliant, its movements quick and decisive. You hear its emphatic chirp, and see it dart swiftly beneath or through the branches that reach out over the creek.

It nests upon the ground, or amid the roots of an upturned tree in the woods near the water that it haunts. Every season for many years I have looked for the nest, but failed to find it till last summer.

My son and I were camping in the Catskills, when one day, as I was slowly making my way down one of those limpid trout streams, I saw a water-thrush dart from out a pile of logs and driftwood that the floods had left on the margin of the stream. The bird at once betrayed much anxiety, and I knew the nest was near.

I proceeded carefully to explore the pile of driftwood, and especially the roots of an upturned tree which it held. I went over the mass almost inch by inch several times. There was a little cavern in it, a yard or more deep, where the light was dim; a translucent pool of water formed the floor of it, and kept me from passing its threshold. I suspected the nest was in there amid the roots or broken branches, but my eye failed to detect it.

"I will go on with my fishing," I said, "and return to-morrow and lay siege to this secret."

So on the morrow I returned, and carefully secreted myself on a mossy bank a few yards from the pile of driftwood. Presently the parent bird came with food in its beak, but instantly spying me, though I fancied that in my recumbent position and faded gray clothes I simulated well an old log, she grew alarmed and refused to approach the nest.

She flitted nervously about from point to point, her attention directed to me, and uttering a sharp, chiding note. Soon her mate came, and the two birds flitted about me, peering, attitudinizing, scolding. The mother bird is always the bolder and more demonstrative on such occasions. I was amused at her arts and feints and her sudden fits of alarm. Sometimes she would quickly become silent, and stealthily approach the entrance of the little cavern in the pile of driftwood; then, her fears and suspicions reviving, with emphatic chirps she would try again to penetrate the mystery of that motionless, prostrate form on the bank.

The dead branch of a tree that slanted down to the bed of the stream near me was her favorite perch. Inch by inch she would hop up it, her body moving like a bandmaster's baton, her notes sharp and emphatic, her wings slightly drooping, meanwhile bringing first one eye and then the other to bear upon the supposed danger.

While she was thus engaging my attention, I saw the male quickly slip into the little cavern with

194

loaded beak, and in a moment reappear. He ran swiftly along the dry pebbles a few yards, and then took to wing, and joined in the cry against me. In a few moments he disappeared, presumably in quest of more food.

The mother, after many feints and passes and false moves, half-fearful of her own rashness, darted into the little cavern also. She soon shot out from it on nimble foot, as had her mate, then took to wing, and to fresh peering and abuse of the strange object on the bank.

The male was soon on the scene again, and after a little flourishing, entered the shadow of the cavern as before. Pausing a moment, the female did the same.

Evidently their suspicions were beginning to be lulled. They had seen fishermen many, a few every day for weeks, and had grown used to them; these had gone on about their business ; but this one that tarried and seemed bent on finding out other people's business, — here was cause for alarm!

In less than half an hour I felt sure I had the birds' secret, — I had seen in the recesses of the cavern the exact spot where they seemed to pause a moment and then turn back. So I approached the spot confidently ; I got down on my knees and charged my eyes to find the nest.

I am surprised that they seem baffled. At the particular niche or shelf in the mass of roots they report only moss or moist stones, — no nest there. I peer long and long. The little pool of limpid water keeps me five or six feet away.

Well, there must be some unseen hole or cavity in there which leads to the nest beyond the reach of the eye. But I will watch again and be sure. So I retreat to the bank, and the same little comedy or drama is played as before.

At last I am positive I can put my hand upon the nest. I procure a fragment of a board, bridge over the little pool, thrust my head into the dim light of the cavity, and closely scan every inch of the surface. No nest, says the eye. Then I will try another sense; I will feel with my hand.

Slowly my hand explores the place; presently it touches something soft and warm at the very spot where I had seen the birds pause. It is the backs of the young birds; they have flattened themselves down until their beaks are on a level with the top of the nest. They have baffled the eye because, in the scant light, they blend perfectly with their surroundings and just fill the depression of the nest. The hand, going behind form and color, finds them out. I felt that I had penetrated one of the prettiest secrets in all the woods, and got a new glimpse of the art and cunning of a bird.

The young were between down and feather, of a grayish slate color, and they played their part well. At my approach they would settle down in the nest

196

till, instead of five, they became one, and that one a circular mass of dark bluish stone or fragment of bark. When I withdrew or concealed myself, they would rise up and their individual forms become outlined.

Another new nest which it was my luck to find the past summer was that of the worm-eating warbler, a bird of the Carolinian fauna, that heretofore has not been known to breed in our State — New York. It was a new find, then, in a double sense, new to me and new to the ornithology of the State.

One day in early June, as I was walking along a path on the side of a bushy hill, near dense woods, I had a glimpse of a small brown bird that dashed away from the bank but a few feet from me. I took it to be the oven-bird.

Looking to the spot from whence it started, I saw a bird with a striped head standing on the edge of a nest in the side of the shelving bank, with something white in its beak. I saw the heads of the young birds beneath, and took in the situation instantly; I had surprised the mother bird while she was waiting upon her young. She stood motionless, half-turned toward me, still keeping the white mass in her beak.

Neither of us stirred for a minute or two, and the other parent made no sound, though he lingered but a few yards away.

Presently I slowly withdrew, and sat down a few paces away. The male bird now became quite uneasy, and flitted from bush to bush and uttered his alarm chirp. The mother bird never stirred. I could see her loaded beak from where I sat. In two or three minutes she dropped or otherwise disposed of her morsel, but kept her place above her young. Then her mate, taking his cue from her, quieted down and soon disappeared from view.

After long waiting I approached the nest, and pausing ten feet away, regarded it some moments. The bird never stirred. Then I came nearer, and when I sat down within four or five feet of the nest, the bird flew out upon the ground before me, and sought to lure me away by practicing the old confidence game that birds so often resort to on such occasions.

She was seized with incipient paralysis in her members ; she dragged herself about upon the ground; she quivered and tottered and panted with open beak, and seemed on the point of going all to pieces. Seeing this game did not work and that I remained unmoved, she suddenly changed her tactics; she flew up to a limb and gave me a piece of her mind in no equivocal terms. This brought the male, and true to his name, he had a worm in his beak.

Both now joined in the scolding, and the rumpus attracted a vireo to the spot, who came to see what the danger really was. But evidently the warblers regarded his presence as an intrusion.

The nest was in the edge of the bank where the

198

soil was broken away a little, and was mainly composed of dry leaves and pine needles. The young, five in number, were probably a week old.

I came again the next day, and found the bird sitting on the edge of the nest as before, and ready, when I disturbed her, with the same arts to lure me away. I paid frequent visits to the place thereafter till the young had flown.

The song of the male — a little shuffling chant much like that of Chippy — was frequently heard. This warbler may be instantly known by its olivaceous color and the four sharp black stripes on its buff-colored head. It is one of the prettiest and most interesting of the warblers.

VII

AUGUST DAYS

ONE of our well-known poets, in personifying August, represents her as coming with daisies in her hair. But an August daisy is a sorry affair; it is little more than an empty, or partly empty, seed-vessel. In the Northern States the daisy is in her girlhood and maidenhood in June; she becomes very matronly early in July, — fat, faded, prosaic, — and by or before August she is practically defunct. I recall no flower whose career is more typical of the life, say, of the average European peasant woman, or of the women of barbarous tribes, its grace and youthfulness pass so quickly into stoutness, obesity, and withered old age. How positively girlish and taking is the daisy during the first few days of its blooming, while its snow-white rays yet stand straight up and shield its tender centre somewhat as a hood shields a girl's face! Presently it becomes a perfect disk and bares its face to the sun; this is the stage of its young womanhood. Then its yellow centre — its body — begins to swell and become gross, the rays slowly turn brown, and finally wither up and drop. It is a flower no longer, but a receptacle packed with ripening seeds.

A relative of the daisy, the orange-colored hawk-weed (*Hieracium aurantiacum*), which within the past twenty years has spread far and wide over New York and New England, is often at the height of its beauty in August, when its deep vivid orange is a delight to the eye. It repeats in our meadows and upon our hilltops the flame of the columbine of May, intensified. The personified August with these flowers in her hair would challenge our admiration and not our criticism. Unlike the daisy, it quickly sprouts again when cut down with the grass in the meadows, and renews its bloom. Parts of New England, at least, have a native August flower quite as brilliant as the hawkweed just described, and far less a usurper; I refer to meadow-beauty, or rhexia, found near the coast, which suggests a purple evening primrose.

Nature has, for the most part, lost her delicate tints in August. She is tanned, hirsute, freckled, like one long exposed to the sun. Her touch is strong and vivid. The coarser, commoner wayside flowers now appear, — vervain, eupatorium, mimulus, the various mints, asters, golden-rod, thistles, fireweed, mulleins, motherwort, catnip, blueweed, turtle-head, sunflowers, clematis, evening primrose, lobelia, gerardia, and, in the marshes of the lower Hudson, marshmallows, and vast masses of the purple loosestrife. Mass and intensity take the place of delicacy and furtiveness. The spirit of Nature has grown bold and aggressive; it is rank and coarse; she flaunts her weeds in our faces. She wears a thistle on her bosom. But I must not forget the delicate rose gerardia, which she also wears upon her bosom, and which suggests that, before the season closes, Nature is getting her hand ready for her delicate spring flora. With me this gerardia lines open paths over dry knolls in the woods, and its little purple bells and smooth, slender leaves form one of the most exquisite tangles of flowers and foliage of the whole summer. It is August matching the color and delicacy of form of the fringed polygala of May. I know a half-wild field bordering a wood, which is red with strawberries in June and pink with gerardia in August.

One may still gather the matchless white pond-lily in this month, though this flower is in the height of its glory earlier in the season, except in the northern lakes.

A very delicate and beautiful marsh flower that may be found on the borders of lakes in northern New York and New England is the horned bladder-wort, — yellow, fragrant, and striking in form, like a miniature old-fashioned bonnet, when bonnets covered the head and projected beyond the face, instead of hovering doubtfully above the scalp. The horn curves down and out like a long chin from a face hidden within the bonnet. I have found this rare flower in the Adirondacks and in Maine. It may doubtless be found in Canada, and in Michigan and Wisconsin. Britton and Brown say " south to Florida and Texas." It is the most fragrant August flower known to me. This month has not many fragrant flowers to boast of. Besides the above and the pond-lily I recall two others, — the small purple fringed-orchis and a species of lady's-tresses (*Spiranthes cernua*).

The characteristic odors of August are from fruit — grapes, peaches, apples, pears, melons — and the ripening grain; yes, and the blooming buckwheat. Of all the crop and farm odors this last is the most pronounced and honeyed, rivaling that of the flowering locust of May and of the linden in July.

The mistakes of our lesser poets in dealing with nature themes might furnish me with many a text in this connection. Thus one of them makes the call of the phœbe-bird prominent in August. One would infer from the poem that the phœbe was not heard during any other month. Now it is possible that the poet heard the phœbe in August, but if so, the occurrence was exceptional, and it is more probable that it was the wood pewee that he heard. The phœbe is most noticeable in April and early May, and its characteristic call is not often heard till the sun is well up in the sky. Most of our song-birds are silent in August, or sing only fitfully, as do the song sparrow and the oriole. The real August song-ster, and the bird that one comes to associate with the slow, drowsy days, is the indigo-bird. After midsummer its song, delivered from the top of some small tree in the pasture or a bushy field, falls upon the ear with a peculiar languid, midsummery effect. The boys and girls gathering raspberries and black-berries hear it; the stroller through the upland fields, or lounger in the shade of maple or linden, probably hears no bird-song but this, if he even distinguishes this from the more strident insect voices. The plum-age of the bird is more or less faded by this time, the vivid indigo of early June is lightly brushed with a dull sooty shade, but the song is nearly as full as the earlier strain, and in the dearth of bird voices is even more noticeable. I do not now recall that any of our poets have embalmed this little cerulean song-ster in their verse.

One may also occasionally hear the red-eyed vireo in August, but it is low tide with him too. His song has a reminiscent air, like that of the indigo. The whip-poor-will calls fitfully in this month, and may be heard even in September; but he quickly checks himself, as if he knew it was out of season. In the Adirondacks I have heard the speckled Canada warbler in August, and the white-throated sparrow. But nearly all the migratory birds begin to get rest-less during this month. They cut loose from their nesting-haunts and drift through the woods in pro-

miscuous bands, and many of them start on their
southern journey. From my woods along the Hudson the warblers all disappear before the middle of
the month.* Some of them are probably in hiding
during the moulting season. The orioles begin to
move south about the middle of the month, and by
the first of September the last of them have passed.
They occasionally sing in a suppressed tone during
this migration, probably the young males trying their
instruments. It is at this time, when full of frolic
and mischief, like any other emigrants with faces
set to new lands, that they make such havoc in the
Hudson River vineyards. They seem to puncture
the grapes in the spirit of pure wantonness, or as if
on a wager as to who can puncture the most. The
swallows — the cliff and the barn — all leave in
August, usually by the 20th, though the swift may
be seen as late as October. I notice that our poets
often detain the swallows much beyond the proper
date. One makes them perch upon the barn in October. Another makes them noisy about the eaves
in Indian summer. An English poet makes the swallow go at November's bidding. The tree swallow may
often be seen migrating in countless numbers along
the coast in early October, but long ere this date the
barn and the cliff swallows are in tropical climes.
They begin to flock, and apparently rehearse the
migrating programme, in July.

The bobolinks go in early August with the red-shouldered starlings, and along the Potomac and Chesapeake Bay become the reed-birds of sportsmen. One often hears them in this month calling from high in the air as they journey southward from more northern latitudes.

About the most noticeable bird of August in New York and New England is the yellowbird, or goldfinch. This is one of the last birds to nest, seldom hatching its eggs till late in July. It seems as if a particular kind of food were required to rear its brood, which cannot be had at an earlier date. The seed of the common thistle is apparently its mainstay. There is no prettier sight at this season than a troop of young goldfinches, led by their parents, going from thistle to thistle along the roadside and pecking the ripe heads to pieces for the seed. The plaintive call of the young is one of the characteristic August sounds. Their nests are frequently destroyed, or the eggs thrown from them, by the terrific July thunder-showers. Last season a pair had a nest on the slender branch of a maple in front of the door of the house where I was staying. The eggs were being deposited, and the happy pair had many a loving conversation about them many times each day, when one afternoon a very violent storm arose which made the branches of the trees stream out like wildly disheveled hair, quite turning over those on the windward side, and emptying the pretty nest of its eggs. In such cases the birds build anew,

— a delay that may bring the incubation into August. Such an accident had probably befallen a pair of which I one season made this note in my note-book, under date of August 6: —

"A goldfinches' nest in the maple-tree near the window where I write, the female sitting on four pale bluish-white eggs ; the male feeds her on the nest ; whenever she hears his voice she calls incessantly, much after the manner of the young birds, — the only case I recall of the sitting bird calling while in the act of incubation. The male evidently brings the food in his crop, or at least well back in his beak or throat, as it takes him several moments to deliver it to his mate, which he does by separate morsels. The male, when disturbed by a rival, utters the same note as he pursues his enemy from point to point that the female does when calling to him. It does not sound like a note of anger, but of love and confidence."

As the bird-songs fail, the insect harpers and fiddlers begin. August is the heyday of these musicians. The katydid begins to "work her chromatic reed" early in the month, and with her comes that pulsing, purring monotone of the little pale tree-crickets. These last fill the August twilight with a soft, rhythmic undertone of sound, which forms a sort of background for the loud, strident notes of the katydids.

August, too, is the month of the screaming, high-sailing hawks. The young are now fully fledged, and they love to circle and scream far above the mountain's crest all the tranquil afternoon. Sometimes one sees them against the slowly changing and swelling thunder-heads that so often burden the horizon at this season.

It is on the dewy August mornings that one notices the webs of the little spiders in the newly mown meadows. They look like gossamer napkins spread out upon the grass, — thousands of napkins far and near. The farmer looks upon it as a sign of rain; but the napkins are there every day; only a heavier dew makes them more pronounced one morning than another.

Along the paths where my walks oftenest lead me in August, in rather low, bushy, wet grounds, the banner flower is a species of purple boneset, or trumpet-weed, so called, I suppose, because its stem is hollow. It often stands up seven or eight feet high, crowned with a great mass of dull purple bloom, and leads the ranks of lesser weeds and plants like a great chieftain. Its humbler servitors are white boneset and swamp milkweed, while climbing boneset trails its wreaths over the brookside bushes not far away. A much more choice and brilliant purple, like some invasion of metropolitan fashion into a rural congregation, is given to a near-by marsh by the purple loosestrife. During the latter half of August the bog is all aflame with it. There is a wonderful style about this plant, either singly or in masses. Its suggestion is as distinctly feminine as that of the trumpet-weed is masculine.

When the poet personifies August, let him fill her arms with some of these flowers, or place upon her brows a spray of wild clematis, which during this month throws its bridal wreaths so freely over our bushy, unkempt waysides and fence corners. After you have crowned and adored your personified August in this way, then give the finishing touch with the scarlet raceme of the cardinal flower, flaming from the sheaf of ranker growths in her arms. How this brilliant bit of color, glassing itself in a dark, still pool, lights up and affects the vague, shadowy background upon which it is projected!

In August the "waters blossom." This is the term the country people in my section apply to a phenomenon which appears in the more sluggish streams and ponds during this month. When examined closely, the water appears to be filled with particles of very fine meal. I suspect, though I do not know, that these floating particles are the spores of some species of fresh-water alga; or they may be what are called zoöspores. The algæ are at their rankest during August. Great masses of some species commonly called "frogs' spawn" rise to the surface of the Hudson and float up and down with the tide, — green unclean-looking masses, many yards in extent. The dog-star seems to invoke these fermenting masses from the deep. They suggest decay, but they are only the riot of the lower forms of vegetable life.

August, too, is the month of the mushrooms, — those curious abnormal flowers of a hidden or subterranean vegetation, invoked by heat and moisture from darkness and decay as the summer wanes. Do they not suggest something sickly and uncanny in Nature? her unwholesome dreams and night fancies, her pale superstitions; her myths and legends and occult lore taking shape in them, spectral and fantastic, at times hinting something libidinous and unseemly: vegetables with gills, fibreless, bloodless; earth-flesh, often offensive, unclean, immodest, often of rare beauty and delicacy, of many shades and colors — creamy white, red, yellow, brown, — now the hue of an orange, now of a tomato, now of a potato, some edible, some poisonous, some shaped like spread umbrellas, some like umbrellas reversed by the wind, — the sickly whims and fancies of Nature, some imp of the earth mocking and travestying the things of the day. Under my evergreens I saw a large white disk struggling up through the leaves and the débris like the full moon through clouds and vapors. This simile is doubtless suggested to my mind by a line of a Southern poet, Madison Cawein, which I look upon as one of the best descriptive lines in recent nature poetry: —

" The slow toadstool comes bulging, moony white,
Through loosening loam.''

Sometimes this moon of the loam is red, or golden,
or bronzed; or it is so small that it suggests only a
star. The shy wood folk seem to know the edible
mushrooms, and I notice often eat away the stalk
and nibble at the top or pileus.

One day two friends came to see me with something wrapped up in their handkerchiefs. They said
they had brought their dinner with them, — they
had gathered it in the woods as they came along,
— beefsteak mushrooms. The beefsteak was duly
cooked and my friends ate of it with a relish. A portion was left, which my dog attacked rather doubt-
ingly, and then turned away from, with the look of
one who has been cheated. Mock-meat, that is what
it was, — a curious parody upon a steak, as the dog
soon found out. I know a man who boasts of having identified and eaten seventy-five different species. When the season is a good one for mushrooms,
he snaps his fingers at the meat trust, even going to
the extent of drying certain kinds to be used for
soup in the winter.

The decay of a mushroom parodies that of real
flesh, — a kind of unholy rotting ending in black-
ness and stench. Some species imitate jelly, — mock
calves'-foot jelly, which soon melts down and becomes an uncanny mass. Occasionally I see a blue-

A Group of Mushrooms

gilled mushroom, — an infusion of indigo in its cells. How forbidding it looks! Yesterday in the August woods I saw a tiny mushroom like a fairy parasol of a Japanese type, — its top delicately fluted.

During the steaming, dripping, murky, and muggy dog-days that sometimes come the latter half of August, how this fungus growth runs riot in the woods and in the fields too, — a kind of sacrilegious vegetation mocking Nature's saner and more wholesome handiwork, — the flowers of death, vegetable spectres.

August days are for the most part tranquil days; the fret and hurry of the season are over. We are on the threshold of autumn. Nature dreams and meditates; her veins no longer thrill with the eager, frenzied sap; she ripens and hardens her growths; she concentrates; she begins to make ready for winter. The buds for next year are formed during this month, and her nuts and seeds and bulbs finish storing up food for the future plant.

From my outlook upon the Hudson the days are placid, the river is placid, the boughs of the trees gently wag, the bees make vanishing-lines through the air. The passing boats create a great commotion in the water, converting it from a cool, smooth, shadowy surface to one pulsing and agitated. The pulsations go shoreward in long, dark, rolling, glassy swells. The grapes are purpling in the vineyard; the apples and pears are coloring in the orchard;

the corn is glazing in the field; the oats are ripe for the cradle; grasshoppers poise and shuffle above the dry road; yellow butterflies mount upward face to face; thistledown drifts by on the breeze; a sparrow sings fitfully now and then; dusty wheelmen go by on their summer vacation tours; boats appear upon the river loaded with gay excursionists, and on every hand the stress and urge of life have abated.

VIII

BABES IN THE WOODS

ONE day in early May, Ted and I made an expedition to the Shattega, a still, dark, deep stream that loiters silently through the woods not far from my cabin. As we paddled along, we were on the alert for any bit of wild life of bird or beast that might turn up. Ted was especially on the lookout for birds'-nests, and many times I pushed the boat up close to the bank that he might explore with his slender arm the cavities the woodpeckers had made in the dead tree trunks that bordered or overhung the stream. Only once did he bring out a handful of material that suggested a bird's-nest, and on examining it, sure enough, there was a bird's egg, the egg of the chickadee. The boy had clutched the nest, egg and all, and had made such a wreck of the former that we concluded it was useless to try to restore it and return it to the cavity. So Ted added the egg to his collection, and, I suspect, regretted the result of his eager dive into the hollow stub less than I did.

There were so many of these abandoned woodpecker chambers in the small dead trees as we went along that I determined to secure the section of a tree

215

containing a good one to take home and put up for the bluebirds. " Why don't the bluebirds occupy them here ? " inquired Ted. " Oh," I replied, " bluebirds do not come so far into the woods as this. They prefer nesting-places in the open, and near human habitations." After carefully scrutinizing several of the trees, we at last saw one that seemed to fill the bill. It was a small dead tree trunk seven or eight inches in diameter, that leaned out over the water, and from which the top had been broken. The hole, round and firm, was ten or twelve feet above us. After considerable effort I succeeded in breaking the stub off near the ground, and brought it down into the boat. " Just the thing," I said ; " surely the blue-birds will prefer this to an artificial box." But, lo and behold, it already had bluebirds in it! We had not heard a sound or seen a feather till the trunk was in our hands, when, on peering into the cavity, we discovered two young bluebirds about half grown. This was a predicament indeed! My venture had proved to be more rash and regretta-ble than Ted's.

Well, the only thing we could do was to stand the tree trunk up again as well as we could, and as near as we could to where it had stood before. This was no easy thing. But after a time we had it fairly well replaced, one end standing in the mud of the shallow water and the other resting against a tree. This left the hole to the nest about ten feet below and to one side of its former position. Just then we heard the voice of one of the parent birds, and we quickly paddled to the other side of the stream, fifty feet away, to watch her proceedings, saying to each other, "Too bad," "Too bad." The mother bird had a large beetle in her beak. She alighted upon a limb a few feet above the former site of her nest, looked down upon us, uttered a note or two, and then dropped down confidently to the point in the vacant air where the entrance to her nest had been but a few moments before. Here she hovered on the wing a second or two, looking for something that was not there, and then returned to the perch she had just left, apparently not a little disturbed. She hammered the beetle rather excitedly upon the limb a few times, as if it were in some way at fault, then dropped down to try for her nest again. Only vacant air there! She hovers and hovers, her blue wings flickering in the checkered light; surely that precious hole *must* be there; but no, again she is baffled, and again she returns to her perch, and mauls the poor beetle till it must be reduced to a pulp. Then she makes a third attempt, then a fourth, and a fifth, and a sixth, till she becomes very much excited. "What could have happened? am I dreaming? has that beetle hoodooed me?" she seems to say, and in her dismay she lets the bug drop, and looks bewilderedly about her. Then she flies away through the woods, calling. "Going for her mate," I said to

Ted. "She is in deep trouble, and she wants sympathy and help."

In a few minutes we heard her mate answer, and presently the two birds came hurrying to the spot, both with loaded beaks. They perched upon the familiar limb above the site of the nest, and the mate seemed to say, "My dear, what has happened to you? I can find that nest." And he dived down, and brought up in the empty air just as the mother had done. How he winnowed it with his eager wings! how he seemed to bear on to that blank space! His mate sat regarding him intently, confident, I think, that he would find the clew. But he did not. Baffled and excited, he returned to the perch beside her. Then she tried again, then he rushed down once more, then they both assaulted the place, but it would not give up its secret. They talked, they encouraged each other, and they kept up the search, now one, now the other, now both together. Sometimes they dropped down to within a few feet of the entrance to the nest, and we thought they would surely find it. No, their minds and eyes were intent only upon that square foot of space where the nest had been. Soon they withdrew to a large limb many feet higher up, and seemed to say to themselves, "Well, it is not there, but it must be here somewhere; let us look about." A few minutes elapsed, when we saw the mother bird spring from her perch and go straight as an arrow to the nest.

Her maternal eye had proved the quicker. She had found her young. Something like reason and common-sense had come to her rescue; she had taken time to look about, and behold! there was that precious doorway. She thrust her head into it, then sent back a call to her mate, then went farther in, then withdrew. "Yes, it is true, they are here, they are here!" Then she went in again, gave them the food in her beak, and then gave place to her mate, who, after similar demonstrations of joy, also gave them his morsel.

Ted and I breathed freer. A burden had been taken from our minds and hearts, and we went cheerfully on our way. We had learned something, too; we had learned that when in the deep woods you think of bluebirds, bluebirds may be nearer you than you think.

The young rabbits I saw one day in early May on the edge of a clearing in the woods suggested babies quite as much as the bluebirds did. The mother had come out of the cover of the rocks and bushes and made her nest on a dry knoll in the edge of a muck swamp where the ground had been cleared only a week or two before. The man at work with the grubbing-hoe came near striking into the nest, when the young sprang out. He caught them and put them back under their cover and resumed his work in another place. In the afternoon I happened that way. He told me what he had found, and pointed to the spot a few yards off. I approached the place cautiously and began to scan the ground at my feet. There was no bush or stump or weed or stone to distract my eye, — only the back of a small knoll, brown with fern stubble and dry fern leaves.

"I can see no nest or rabbits here," I said to George. "Where are they?" So he came up, and stooping over, lifted up a tiny coverlid of dry fern stalks, in which were mingled tufts of gray hair, and disclosed a small depression in the ground, where sat three little rabbits that one might almost have held in the palm of his hand. Their ears were depressed, their eyes shone, and their hearts beat fast. In a moment they sprang out; we covered them with our hats and hands, and restored them to the nest as gently as we could, pulling their blanket over them. But they pushed their heads up through it and between our fingers in their efforts to escape. We held them down and finally quieted them, and then carefully withdrew. I do not know how long they remained in the nest, but when I came the next day with some friends, we found the nest empty. One of my friends, who was a naturalist, picked up the cover of ferns and hair and examined it, and let it fall in pieces to the ground. The weather was very warm; we fancied the mother had taken her family into the bush. A night or two after was very cold, with heavy frost. The day following I again passed the nest, and was surprised to see two little rabbits sitting side by side in it. As they did not move, I touched them, and found them dead and cold. The mother, on the approach of the cold wave, had evidently brought her young back to the nest, and having no cover over them, they had perished of the frost. One would have thought she would stay by them to keep them warm, or else cover them with the fragments of the old blanket. Though of course it is possible that she herself had fallen a victim to some enemy, and that the young had died of hunger, seeking in their last extremity the cradle in which they were born. The fate of the third one I do not know. I left the two babies in the nest as I had found them.

On the third day I came that way again with Ted. To my surprise, the two baby rabbits had disappeared. But what was that sticking up through the soil in the bottom of the cavity? It was the end of one tiny ear, and beneath it we found the two young rabbits carefully buried. We exhumed them and brought them forth. They had been literally buried. What or who had performed these last sad rites? The mother? I know not. Not a hair of them had been injured, as far as we could see, but the little bodies had been carefully put from sight, not by the use of leaves, as the robins covered the children in the nursery tale, but by soil. We replaced them in their double grave and went on our way.

It has since occurred to me that this burying was probably the work of a species of beetle, which removed the ground beneath them, letting the bodies settle into the earth.

IX

A LOST FEBRUARY

WE lost February and found August, for Jamaica is a country cursed with perpetual summer. In four days we steamed straight through two seasons. When we left Philadelphia on the 30th of January, 1902, the rigors of midwinter were upon us, a typical northeast snowstorm was settling down to its best work, the mercury was low in the teens, the ship's decks were piled with snow, and the friends that came to see us off shivered in their warmest wraps. The steamer made her way slowly through the drifting ice and sodden snow sheets that covered the Delaware, and did not reach the clear waters of the bay till night had fallen.

The next day winter seemed far behind us. We were in May; the day after we ran into June, and the shade of the awnings began to be acceptable; the third day we were in July; the captain blossomed out in his white duck suit; we sought the shade of the ship eagerly; on the fourth day it was August, and August it continued all the while that we were in Jamaica.

On the third day, in the July weather, as I came

up on deck in the morning, I caught my first sight of tropic seas, — emerald, indigo, violet, blending and shifting there over the surface of the placid water, and suggesting some realm of fable and romance.

What are those white birds that go in loose flocks, skimming the surface of the water, then suddenly disappearing? a snowbird where snow never falls? Then, as more appear, it suddenly dawns upon me that I am seeing my first flying-fish. No bird has such a strenuous, machine-like flight as that. I am on the shady side of the ship, and the afternoon sun, falling upon the winged fishes, makes them, against the deep blue of the sea, appear almost snow white. Every few minutes, one or two, or a dozen, would suddenly break from the water and go spinning away from the ship as straight as arrows, striking the water again several hundred feet away. It is not the flight of a bird but of a toy machine, something wound up and, if rightly launched, calculated to go fifty or one hundred yards in a right line. It is a *tour de force.* There is no freedom or mastery in it as in a bird's flight. It reminds one of the excursions of certain persons into poetry, — my own, for instance. How determined it is! but how restricted and mechanical! Sometimes the flyer would suddenly collapse after a few feet, as if it had not launched itself at just the right angle. Often it would cut through the crests of the small waves, never swerving from a right line. No power to swoop, or soar, or ride the air; scales instead of feathers; fins in lieu of quills; a creature out of its element, making surprising head-way there for a brief moment; very pretty and novel, but, I fancy, showing none of the grace and mastery that it does beneath the wave. At night one fell upon the deck of the ship, caught up and car-ried there, the officer said, by a gust of wind. I think an ingenious person might construct a tin fish with wings that would spin through the air in much the same way.

The flight of the fish is evidently its play, and not its serious business in life, though it is suggested that it is also a means of enabling it to escape its enemies. These fish seemed on this occasion to be racing with one another, like the dolphins, or as if on a wager as to which could stay in the air the longest and cover the greatest distance.

If, in the evolution of animal life upon the globe, the birds emerged from the fishes and reptiles, as the biologists teach, is this sport of the flying-fish all that now remains of the grand impulse that brought about that transformation ? An upward striving of the creative energy that changed scales into feathers, and fins into wings, and peopled the air with the thousand forms of bird life, now surviving only in this pretty and odd freak of the flying-fish ?

On the fourth day, in the midsummer tempera-ture, we began to thread our way amid the tropic or

semi-tropic islands, the Bahamas, — San Salvador
there dimly seen on our right, and, later, Crooked
Island in fuller view upon our left. Soon the mountains of Cuba were dim shadows there to the west
of us, and on the morning of the fifth day, the Blue
Mountains of Jamaica were dimly seen on the
southern horizon. A few hours later they stood up
like larger Catskills, presenting, in their higher
peaks, much the same outlines.

The harbor of Port Antonio, which we entered in
mid-afternoon, is like a pocket in a woman's dress;
you would never suspect its presence. Tucked away
in one of the folds of the mountainous coast, it
makes no sign till the bow of the ship begins to poke
its way in. Small and cozy and picturesque, as I
looked down at the water against the steamer's
side, it seemed as blue and opaque as blue paint.
The dense, stiff, shining foliage of the vegetation
upon the slopes about us and the rows of cocoanut
palms upon the beach were novel sights to northern
eyes.

How absurd seemed the woolen blankets and over-
coats we were obliged to carry to our lodging-house.
We spent but one night in Port Antonio, in a clean
lodging-house kept by a Canadian family lately
from New Brunswick. I shall not soon forget a slender, solemn-faced little girl of five or six years, who
followed me about, eying me very seriously and intently, till she finally said: "I know you are Santa

Claus, are n't you? I know you are, and I 'm going
to tell you what I want. I want a cradle for my dolly
and a new hat and a little gold watch," — all this
said very slowly and solemnly, and with a sort of
hushed, awed air, closely watching my face the while.
I saw the child was in dead earnest, so I told her I
was not Santa Claus. "Yes, you are, I know you
are," she replied. "Will you bring me these things?
I should like them now. Is your pack here?" I
could not shake her off, and finally had to tell her
that my pack was on the steamer, and that I would
see her in the morning if it contained the things
she wanted. Poor child! her faith in Santa Claus,
and her belief that she had at last caught him, was
pathetic.

The next morning we took the train to Kingston,
going second class as we should have done in England. A colored conductor, colored brakemen, and
colored station agents were novelties to us.

Here is a glimpse of a winter day, February 5,
in Kingston : "I am sitting on a veranda, shut off
from the street by a high brick wall pierced by a
tall gate, and flanked by a parched flower garden
where a few roses only are in bloom. No rain to
speak of since last fall. An atmosphere like that
of our August. Mercury 82°; soft, familiar clouds
slowly drifting over a blue midsummer sky. Turkey buzzards sailing, forever sailing, far and near ;
their shadows sweep across the low roofs of the

houses. Many swifts — the palm swift — diving in
the air, — smaller and more nimble of wing than
our swift. The low gray shingle roofs of the houses
visible on all hands ; women constantly passing in
the streets with trays or baskets on their heads
loaded with fruit, or yams, or cooked food, or other
wares, and sounding their shrill, wild street cries.
Can't understand one of them. Now a yellow man
with a push-cart with some cooling drink goes by.
It seems as if a large percentage of the population
must be on the street peddling, — all negroes. Then
comes the familiar hum and grind of the trolley
cars. Fleet-footed lizards dart here and there in the
shrubbery, or on the garden wall. A large green
one with a purple tail. The Blue Mountains back
of New Castle stand up against the sky, their tops
muffled in clouds. Occasionally a mass of cloud
drifts out toward the plain below and lets down thin
sheets of rain, but does not come far. The arid plain
seems to dissipate it or drive it back."

To escape from the tourist-infested portion of the
island and to get a taste of its wilder interior, we
engaged a carriage and driver, and set out early one
morning along the superb road that leads to Spanish
Town and thence on to Bog Walk and Ewarton.

The road was smooth and hard but dusty, and
the vegetation on either side — vines, bushes, trees,
often forming a solid impenetrable wall — was pow-
dered with dust as in midsummer at home. The

most common vine by the roadside everywhere in Jamaica is a wild morning-glory of many colors, similar to our own, but growing far more luxuriantly, and the crimson bougainvillea.

As you pass along the country highways, you come to have a half-defined feeling that some time in the past there must have been a huge greenhouse here that has gone to decay, and that the plants and shrubs and vines have all escaped and gone wild, invading the fields and woods, and running over the banks and fences. Tender exotics that one sees at home carefully nursed in the windows by our women are here the common weeds by the roadside.

This trip into the interior lasted five days, taking us through the wilder, ruggeder portions of the island for about eighty miles, ending on the railroad at Balaclava. It brought us pretty close to the real life of the people, and, a few times, a little closer to wild nature than was conducive to our comfort. Touch Nature too familiarly here, — sit down by the roadside, or recline under a tree, — and she peppers you with a kind of live pepper in the shape of minute ticks, called also grass lice, that penetrate your clothing and make you burn and itch, until by the aid of your companions you have removed the last adhesive speck from your skin. These living germs take root very quickly, and if left, grow to the size of a small bean. They prey upon the cattle and other live-stock. One could see them on the under, less hairy parts of the cows, looking like large warts. We often saw a large black bird, the kling-kling, perched on the backs of the cattle, making a meal off these gorged ticks. One day one of our party made an excursion of a few rods into the bush, and returned with his coat skirts brown with these dust-like torments. Some colored girls who chanced to be passing came to our aid, and helped whip the ticks off with a certain leafy shrub that they said was death to them. No, you cannot make love to Nature in the tropics as you can in our zone. Beware how you embrace her. She is a lousy beggar, a stinging reptile, a brazen wanton, or a barbaric princess, — just as you happen to find her. Ah, me! even at her best she has not the constancy, the tenderness, the self-forgetfulness, of the Nature of more temperate climes. I must make one exception: these Jamaican streams and rivers, beautiful with the beauty of the purest mountain brooks, have nothing suggestive of the tropics about them; one's heart goes out to them at once. Theirs are the clear, shining faces of old friends, of many a trout camp in the Catskills and Adirondack woods. Limpid and pure as melted snow, no sediment, no earth stain, the pebbles and boulders with which they are paved are washed and scoured as if yesterday had been a day of purification with them; they lack only the coolness of our very best mountain streams.

One would stoop in his thirst to drink from a copious limpid spring gushing out of the mountain-side, but experience a feeling of surprise, if not of repugnance, to find the water as warm as in a bathing-pool. This cannot be the true source, you half think; the water must have been flowing a long way in the sun somewhere. One is apt to forget that the temperature of a spring represents, pretty nearly, the average yearly temperature of a locality. They have a way in Jamaica of reducing the temperature of the drinking-water many degrees by letting it drip slowly through a porous earthen vessel into a pitcher beneath it. Treated thus, one soon comes to regard it as very satisfactory.

Our course that first day soon brought us to the Rio Cobre, along the rocky banks of which the road leisurely took its way to Bog Walk. All the most pleasing features of a clear, rapid, boulder-strewn mountain river, the Rio Cobre presents. The rocks are of limestone, old, worm-eaten, and very picturesque, and the great lucid pools suggested trout and salmon, though they held nothing finer than mullets. On this stream we passed the plant that turns the force of its falls and rapids into electricity, and so furnishes the power that runs the trolley lines in Kingston, twenty miles away.

We passed the night at a lodging-house (no hotels in the country in Jamaica) in Ewarton, and were fairly well cared for by the yellow landlady and her son. The most novel scene I witnessed at Ewarton was that of two old negroes next morning pounding coffee in big mortar-like vessels made out of the trunks of trees. They used a heavy club, and punched and punched and stirred the green coffee to loosen the chaff or skins from the berry, keeping up in the mean time a wild, plaintive chant to which their pounding was timed. They were grizzled and old, and the scene was curious and interesting. Yes, and I recall a famishing dog, scarcely more than a walking skeleton, going about the street licking the ground where a little flour had been spilt.

From Ewarton our course took us over wooded hills and mountains, with here and there a rude clearing, to Chapelton in the valley of the Rio Minho, a distance of about twenty-five miles. My son and Mr. Kellogg, to work off some of their super-fluous American energy, walked the whole distance, fording the Rio Minho a half-dozen or more times in the course of the afternoon. I stuck to the carriage, walking only when I got tired of riding. Bridges are few over these rapid Jamaican streams, but fording them at this season was a trifling matter. On many of the smaller streams, in lieu of a bridge, a wall is built across and the space above it filled in with gravel, resulting in a wide, shallow sheet of water through which carts and pedestrians pass easily, — a new device in road-making to our eyes.

I walked several hours up the valley of the Rio

Minho, a very beautiful stream. A colored boy of twelve, with a singularly sweet face, joined us, and clung closely to me, — a real little comrade. Finally he said: "I like you, it does not tire me to walk with you. When we likes a man, it is fun ;" again, " When we has pleasant company, it makes the way seem short." Later he confessed: "I do love you, and your son, too. When I love a man, I cannot always tell him, but I can tell you." He said he would write me a letter, so I wrote my name and address on a dry bamboo leaf for him. He was a winsome lad, and I shall not soon forget him.

What does one see as he passes along the road in the interior of Jamaica? He sees a superb highway, round and smooth and winding, leading on in front of him, and on either hand bushes and trees and woods; never an open, smooth, cleared field as at home; at best, open glades and long vistas through the groves of logwood and cottonwood. The log-wood groves suggest orchards, — low, branching trees, with curious fluted or beaded trunks and smooth, yellowish, mottled bark, — each tree suggesting a bundle of small columns welded together. The effect was very novel and pretty. The cotton-woods are wide-branching, sturdy-looking trees, like our oaks. Few signs of agriculture as we know it at home are visible; the wattled bamboo huts of the negroes here and there in the bush are surrounded by a few banana or breadfruit or orange trees, with a little patch of half-cultivated yams; there are few cattle, more donkeys, and many black, lean pigs ; colored people on the road everywhere, men, women, and children, — mostly women and children, — with small or large burdens upon their heads, going to their work in the bush or going to and returning from market. The smallest bundle is here carried upon the head.

I think it was this day that I first made the acquaintance of the sensitive plant, — " shame lady," the natives call it. I saw a ball of delicate pink bloom, the size of a boy's marble, amid a mass of small, fine, pinnate leaves by the roadside. I plucked the flower and a branch of the plant with it, when lo! as I turned my eyes from the flower to the leaves, the latter were not the ones I thought I had gathered. I plucked more, and then saw the sudden change in the appearance of the leaves: the moment they were touched they shut up like a book, the two halves hinging on the midrib. You stoop and gather a spray of many-divided small leaves, — you rise up with something in your hand that has an entirely different aspect, the closed leaves presenting only sharp edges to you. Touch the plant with your foot, or stick, ever so gently, and its aspect changes in a twinkling. It is its way of hiding like a sentient thing; the stems drop, the leaves close, but the pretty flower is unchanged. Why so fearful? what is it hiding from? of what advantage is

234

this extreme sensitiveness to it? I could not find out. I noticed that the falling rain did not cause it to shut up. It took it about seven or eight minutes to open its leaves again, which it did very slowly. The plant belongs to the leguminous family. Indeed, Jamaica is a wonderful country for pods and beans. You see pod-bearing trees and bushes everywhere, and pick up on the seacoast huge black beans that look like some rare polished stones. One day we passed dense masses of low trees in bloom by the roadside; they looked like our honey-locust, except that the blossoms were yellow.

On this day we passed through a dry section of the country, where water was scarce; and nearly every colored boy or woman that we met carried a long stick of sugar-cane. This was for drink. We persuaded one boy to part with his six or eight feet of cane, and thereafter for many miles three trav-elers might have been seen eagerly gnawing at the end of a section of the sweet, succulent stalk, and chewing it with an air of placid content. The juice slaked the thirst and was pleasant to the taste. By attending closely to business, one could extract the moisture just about fast enough to meet the hourly wants of the system; so that the gnawing and suck-ing could go on indefinitely, or as long as the cane held out.

By the roadside my son made an excursion into a grove of wild oranges, and brought back a branch of one of the trees with the nest of the little blue quit upon it. The nest was made of dry grasses, and was shaped like a small crook-necked gourd; the neck hooked over the limb so that the entrance to it was on one side of the branch and the body of it below the other side. It was very pretty, and I carried it in the carriage for two days hoping to bring it home with me, but it finally got hopelessly crushed.

We saw no cultivation of the soil to speak of till we reached a large sugar plantation in Judas Vale, — one of the few large sugar estates that are still worked in the island, — called Worthy Park, covering a large, oval, sunken valley several miles across. Here were rich level bottoms covered with the green, corn-like sugar-cane, and here sugar-making and rum-making were being carried on by swarms of negroes, in a large old mill with a huge overshot water-wheel. It all smacked of the picturesque, patriarchal, wasteful times. Things were done on a large scale, but awkwardly, cumbrously: a vast herd of oxen and mules to do the hauling, — six or eight yoke of the former hitched to a huge, heavy dray or wagon hauling sugar-cane and driven wildly by as many men, with much running and yelling; bushers and overseers of high and low degree; the planter himself, a typical colonial Englishman, born on the island, — florid, burly, positive, outspoken, authoritative, dissatisfied, but hospitable to us strangers. The planter showed us through his works from the rollers where the cane was being crushed and pressed to the cribs where the rum was being distilled, and then invited us to his house for luncheon. His men were paid mostly by piece work. He said they were worth little at a stated wage by the day or week.

From Worthy Park we took our way over the mountain toward Chapelton, going down the long, steep, peculiar "Old Woman's Hill" into the valley of the beautiful Rio Minho. We saw flocks of green parrots flying across the hill, — my first sight of a wild bright green bird. When we reached the ford of the Rio Minho, there stood our little green heron, looking very homelike to me.

"How far is it to Chapelton?" we asked of a colored man.

"Far enough, sah."

Several miles farther on we put the question to another man.

"Not too far, sah."

The probable distance in miles to any given place we could never get from a native in Jamaica.

Darkness came on, the team lagged, the road grew hilly, and Chapelton seemed to recede before us. Presently, long after dark, we saw far ahead of us, in what seemed a bend in the road, brilliant lights flashing out. Surely, we said, here is Chapelton, and these are the lamps in the streets or in the windows of the houses. But when we reached the place, how bitter was our disappointment to find that the lights came from huge fireflies! There seemed to be a firefly carnival in that particular spot. When one of these insects passed through or over a tree and sent forth his ray, one could see the foliage distinctly. Photographers say that the light is sufficient to "fog" a plate. It was yet a long, tiresome ride to Chapelton, which we found on a hill above the river — a straggling street of poor, dilapidated houses — about ten o'clock. We succeeded in procuring lodging in a house where, I am sure, some of the odors had kept over from the times of the Spanish occupation, and where the beds were as hard as the middle of the road. I sat in the little stuffy sitting-room, tired and sulky, while my companions higgled with the black landlady about charges. No grass could be had in town for the horses, and these had finally to be taken three miles out to pasture by our driver, Andrew.

In the morning we drew the carriage up in front of the lodging-house on the broad, grassy side of the street to load on our traps. Before the luggage was half on, a colored police officer appeared; with great dignity and solemnity he ordered us to remove the carriage, and asked for our names that he might report us at Kingston for violating a village ordinance. We had technically blockaded the street (though ours seemed the only four-wheeled vehicle in town, and a whole circus caravan could have marched past over the free space), and the law must take cognizance of our offense. How stern and unbending the colored corporal was! No matter if we were Americans and ignorant of the law, the offense was the same, and we must answer at the police court in Kingston. Andrew, the driver, "sassed back," and would not give his name or residence, but I gave our names and the corporal wrote them in his note-book. We hustled the wagon back into the yard, gazed upon curiously by a crowd of men, women, and boys that had gathered, put on the rest of our things, and were off. Before we were out of the village, we met the chief magistrate, a hearty young Englishman, who had heard of our arrival and wished to show Mr. Kellogg some attention. He waved aside the complaint of the police corporal who came up just then, asked us into his office, discussed our proposed route with us, and gave us points, and letters of introduction to police sergeants and others on the road. I saw Andrew offer the police corporal, who had given us a glimpse of the inviolability of village ordinances in Jamaica, some copper coins to drink our health with, but he refused them, and we were off in better humor for Frankfield, distant another day's drive.

It was market day in Chapelton, and the road was lined with women and children and donkeys on their way to dispose of the produce of their little farms.

My son and Mr. Kellogg had gone on ahead of the
carriage, and we found them with their cameras set
up on the farther side of the Rio Minho, waiting to
photograph the women and donkeys as they forded
the stream. The women divined their purpose; a
large squad had collected in front of them, refusing
to be the subjects of a picture till they were paid.
"Give us money; give us money, bucra massa."
One old woman, between sixty and seventy, I should
say, had upon her head a burden that weighed
about as many pounds. I tossed her a penny to
placate her a bit, for she protested the most loudly
of any, and she tried to pick up the coin without
removing her burden, but could not quite do it, so
I got down from the wagon and handed it to her,
and got a graceful curtsy for my pains. Bowing
the head is out of the question with such burdens
as they carry. We bought tangerines and oranges
of the women; still they refused to move on, and
their numbers increased. One old woman had eggs
to sell. I handed one of them to Kellogg, and asked
him if he thought it was fresh. Now Kellogg has a
way of imitating the *yeap* of a young chicken that
deceives the mother hen herself. He shook the egg
and placed it to his ear. Faint but clear came the
distressed *yeap* of the imprisoned chick. I heard
it, and others heard; the old woman heard it,
and, as the cry continued, a curious, surprised, in-
credulous look came over her face. "I fear they are

240

not fresh," said Kellogg, and placed the egg to his ear again with the same result. This was too much for the old woman; with a half-angry, half-alarmed look, she reached forth her hand and said, " Gi' me dat egg," and hurrying it into her basket, hastened into the ford. The others followed, and the boys got the *exposure* they wanted.

About mid-forenoon we overtook a colored man with the inevitable machete, going to his work. We walked with him a mile or more. He was a cheery, bright, companionable sort of a man. His name was John Good. He was going to grub out and clean off a bit of land which he had near the river.

"Are you married, John Good?" I asked.

"No, sah, not yet."

"Have you any children, John?"

"Yes, sah, two."

John was living with the mother of his children, but as yet he had neglected the ceremony of marriage.

We wanted a bath, so John conducted us to a large, beautiful, blue pool in the river, shaded by bamboo, where we had our first Jamaican swim. How delicious the water was, like that of our midsummer trout streams far from their source. John said he would catch us a fish, a mullet, with his hands. The feat seemed impossible in such a large, deep pool, but our black comrade came near doing it. We could see his dark form darting about at the bottom of the pool, like that of a huge muskrat, feeling under rocks and roots of trees, and staying down so long that our lungs ached in sympathy. Only a few days before, he said, he had caught fish there with his hands, but this time he could not bring one to the surface.

We overtook girls and boys who had been to market at Chapelton and were on their way home with lightened burdens, some of them making a journey of fifteen miles each way. How lithe and supple some of the young women were, running and dodging and playing games with the boys as they went along, and never losing the burdens from their heads! A squad of four or five kept with us for many miles. I shall not soon forget their happy faces and bright, playful ways.

At Frankfield we passed the night in a police station, — the first experience of the kind any of us had ever had. There was no lodging-house in the place. We had a letter to the police sergeant, and he took us into their snug, clean quarters, and made us comfortable.

The most interesting sight we saw here was the ruins of an old sugar-mill, — fragments of walls and arches overgrown with vines and trees, and the iron skeleton of a large water-wheel. The date in the wall was 1773. At that time all the slopes and hills about were covered with sugar-cane.

The next day, which was Sunday, we pushed on

up the Rio Minho, often fording the shallow and pellucid stream, falling in with colored men with whom we walked and talked, crossing hills and mountains on an easy grade, on to the home of Colonel Hix, near Kendal. We had a letter to Colonel Hix, and were received by him and his wife with true Jamaican hospitality. The colonel is superintendent of schools for a large section of the island. He had served in our Civil War, and had come to Jamaica from Illinois more than thirty years before, in a very bad way from pulmonary trouble. The climate had healed him, and he was now as well as a man over seventy can reasonably hope to be. He expected to finish his days in Jamaica. His house was aptly named "Cozy," and the hours we spent there are very pleasant to recall. Colored people everywhere in their starched Sunday clothes swarmed in the roads and lanes, going to and from their huts amid the trees and bushes, chatting, laughing, and supplying the human element that this rather rude and broken landscape needed.

The next day we continued our journey westward toward the Cock Pit country and the valley of the Black River, passing through a section where the chief product was ginger. The boys and girls all seemed occupied in peeling ginger roots, and before every hut were little platforms where the roots were drying. We passed a family moving, and apparently carrying all their goods and chattels upon their heads, the women, as usual, having the biggest bundles. Indeed, the number of people everywhere in Jamaica upon the highway was a perpetual surprise to us; at least ten times as many as one would see at home in our most populous country districts. Market day comes several times a week, and everybody seems to go to market with something to sell, — a few shillings' worth of yams and oranges, or bananas, or eggs, or other farm produce. How familiar became the sight of a woman, — dusty, sweating, lean-shanked, but determined, — with her donkey being led by a boy or girl, while she urged it from behind, its huge panniers stuffed with grass and a variety of country products, sometimes pigs and poultry being visible.

This day, for the first time in the island, I saw two smooth, nicely plowed fields on a side-hill, such as one sees at home, — many acres free from bushes and weeds, and apparently under thorough cultivation. I wondered at them much till I learned that they were the property of two of my own countrymen, who were going into ginger farming.

We passed the night at Coleyville with the Rev. Mr. Turner, to whom we had a letter, — a forlorn, ramshackle place, but a hospitable host. Here was this man, a Baptist clergyman in middle life, spending his days in this wilderness amid these rude, ignorant people, ministering to their souls and

244

A Jamaica Road

to their sick bodies as best he could, living in an old musty house with two or three slatternly servants, his wife in Scotland, and his two sons being educated at Cambridge. Another year and a half was to elapse before he could take a vacation to visit them and his native land. His seemed to me a bitter cup, but he was not making wry faces over it. Let me again draw upon my note-book: "At Dr. Turner's, Monday, February 10, 4 P. M., 1902. A world of wooded knolls, very primitive. Altitude three thousand feet, mercury 70°, a slow rain falling ; wraiths of fog rising from the woods as at home. Small thatched cabins of the natives here and there visible through the trees. Like our backwoods places, except the curious dumpling-shaped hills scattered on all hands, — no long, sweeping lines and curves.

"The note of the solitaire comes up from the wet woods below us, almost identical with that of the Oregon robin in Alaska, — very pleasing to me. Now a mockingbird alights on a stake a few yards from the house and sings for a moment, — the most abundant songster about here, — not at all a fine songster to me."

In the evening we sat about the table with much talk, while the rain came steadily down. That night we slept three in a bed, — a hard bed and harder pillows. Sleep would not come to me; I charged it to the altitude of three thousand feet; at midnight I crept out, and, wrapped in my blanket, lay upon the floor, — to reduce the altitude, my son said: but no, it was to reduce the problem to simpler terms.

It was foggy and misty when we left Coleyville in the morning, and continued so until we had reduced the altitude by over a thousand feet, and had got below the cloud-line, when at noon, in the valley of Hector's River, we ran into sunshine.

In the afternoon we skirted for two or three hours that curious Cock Pit country, — a vast area covered with huge rough-hewn rocky bowls, several hundred feet deep, and many hundred or even thousand feet across the top, their rims craggy, wooded, their sides and bottoms green and verdurous, usually with a stream or river coming out of the earth on one side, and plunging into it again on the other, — a land of pits and caves and subterranean water-courses. The road, hard and smooth, wound round the rims of these huge pits or bowls, giving us views into the deep, sunken valleys, now on the right hand, now on the left. Now we see a sparkling current, now the hill has swallowed it. The streams come from the earth quietly, gently, and as quietly and gently they return to it. This region is full of caves, one of which, Oxford Cave, near Balaclava, we explored. It was like our own caves, a series of huge irregular chambers, with the inevitable stalactites and stalagmites, and —

what our caves do not have in such numbers —
swarms of bats. The bats came out of the crevices
of the rocks over our heads like bees out of a hive
in swarming time, making a curious soft hum with
their myriad wings. What acute senses of some
kind these creatures must have! In that primal
darkness, when our torches were extinguished, they
would pass and repass us, and thread their way
through those narrow, crooked alleys, without touching a wing to rock or man. The sense which in
the darkness makes us aware of our near approach
to any object, the bat doubtless has in a very acute
and highly developed form.

We found Balaclava one of the most attractive
places we had yet reached. There was a clean, well-
kept lodging-house, where good meals and good
beds could be had at a reasonable charge. We had
contemplated a canoe voyage from near this place
down Black River to the sea, but abandoned the
project. Canoeing or camping out in a tropical
country can have little of the attraction it has amid
our more simple, wholesome, and companionable
nature. From this point we returned to Kingston
by rail, leaving the team to come by the road.

From Kingston one sees the rows of white buildings of New Castle clinging to the shoulders of
the mountain like some new kind of cliff swallow's nests. They have an enticing, adventurous
look. New Castle is the rendezvous of the British

soldiers in Jamaica during the summer. The
military authorities kindly consented to our occupy-
ing a furnished cottage there called " The Refuge,"
which at that season was not in use, — a small,
low, rambling cottage perched upon a shelf of the
mountain, its little flower garden in front full of
blooming roses, geraniums, and heliotrope, and surrounded by a fringe of the ever graceful bamboo.
A thousand feet above us towered Katherine's
Peak; below us we saw the world as a soaring
hawk sees it, the mountains dropping down to the
hills, and the hills to the plain, and the plain, upon
which stands the city of Kingston, tilting to the
sea, twelve or fifteen miles distant, where we saw
the ships sail away into the sky, to the moon, or
to the evening or the morning star. How the sea
rises up into the horizon when viewed from a great
altitude ! We could not tell where the water ended
and the sky began.

We had a colored man, Joseph, whom we had
picked up in Gordonsville, and who served us as
both man and maid, — quiet, willing, modest, reliable Joseph, with broad, naked feet, greatly spread
at the toes, and sturdy neck capable of sustaining
the head, in a climb up the long, steep mountain-
side, with a burden of forty or fifty pounds. We
did not permit Joseph to do the cooking, we liked
that service ourselves, but he gathered the wood, —
mostly dry bamboo, — washed the dishes, and did

errands, one day going to Kingston and back with
great ease.

The climate at this elevation was much like
that of the Catskills in August, or even cooler; the
nights so cool that we could not sit out on the
veranda later than eight o'clock. A double woolen
blanket was not too much covering on the bed.
The whole scenery of the heavens is shifted a little
when you get so far south. The moon passes farther north, Orion and the Pleiades seem right
over head, and the Big Dipper is quite hidden
behind the ridge of Katherine's Peak. Twice
we climbed to the top of the peak along one of the
narrow graded roads called "bridle-paths," that
thread all the valleys and mountain passes in
this island, and find their way, always an easy, leisurely way, to all the mountain summits. In many
places the path was carved out of the soft, crumbling rock. It was lined and draped and cushioned
with mosses and ferns and vines and various tropical growths. Near the top of the mountain two
colored men were clearing it of its various wild
growths with the ubiquitous machete. This tool,
which is carried by nearly every countryman in
Jamaica, is the one universal tool. It serves as a
scythe with which to mow grass, and as an axe to
cut wood and fell trees. It is the tool for tropical
jungles and tangles. With this in his hand, how one
can slash his way through the dense, spiny, vine-

choked thickets! These men were clearing the roads of weeds with it. We saw the light blue wreath of smoke from their fire going up through the dark, glistening green of the forest that clothed the mountain, when we were far below them. Their dog lay curled up by the fire, where something for their dinner was simmering, and barked at us as any other self-respecting dog would have done.

This is the region of the tree ferns, — the only place where we found them, — straight, rough, hairy shafts, five or six inches through, and twelve or fifteen feet high, with a circle of delicate, wide-spreading fronds at the top, — broad, tapering sheets or plumes of green lace crowning a crabbed, touch-me-not-looking column.

On the vertical bank of the roadside, what a wealth of mosses and small ferns and plants! with now and then in the more sunny places a just ripening wild strawberry. We had often to pause and feast our eyes upon this marvelous veil behind which Nature hides her cleft rocks in the tropics. How dark and dense and bearded and choked the forest sweeping down the mountain-side below us, shaggy, glistening, almost scaly, fanged; with touches of rare and delicate beauty, but with an aspect, on the whole, strange, forbidding, treacherous!

When a turn in the path gave us unexpected views across the deep valley upon the huge flank of Blue Mountain Peak, and of its great sweeping skylines, we would pause with delight, and let our eyes go, like falcons loosed for the quarry. From these altitudes we often saw hawks wheeling and heard them screaming far below or above us, just as in summer we are wont to see them from our native mountains, and apparently they were the same species, the red-tailed.

On the summit, which was free of trees, we found our white clover in bloom and the butter-cup and wild strawberries. I was more surprised, however, to find the Scotch gorse blooming here. It can hardly be a native of the island. It was probably brought and planted there by British sol-diers whose summer camp we had just left. It told the story of Tommy Atkins longing for his native hills. He had tried with fair success to create a bit of Scotland there on Katherine's Peak.

From this vantage-ground we could look down upon the coffee plantations tilted up against the mountain-side beneath us. To our eyes they looked like bushy, neglected fields. Here and there we could see what is called a barbecue, — a broad cement platform where the coffee is dried. The superb military road wound leisurely up from the deep valley, — how plainly we could see it, — a yellow ribbon amid the green, looping and loop-ing endlessly. Towards Kingston, vivid emerald squares of sugar-cane held the eye, and suggested fields of Indian corn. They grow our corn in Ja-

251

maica, but only to a very limited extent. We saw ripe corn, and by its side corn just coming up.

On one occasion, my son and I, getting tired of the heat and noises of Kingston, went seeking discomfort, and we found it, the genuine article; but it was the discomfort of campers-out under adverse conditions, — discomfort that time and distance always soften, and, in a measure, transform. Indeed, the woes of campers-out are always better to look back upon than the pleasures of the stay-at-homes. My son, with our traveling companion, Mr. Kellogg, had spent a night at Great Salt Pond, a little side pocket of the Caribbean, beyond Port Henderson, twelve miles distant, where, as the fishermen hauled their nets, he had seen the most wonderful phosphorescent fireworks in the water, and where crocodiles promenaded the shores at midnight. Hither we would go and get a taste of the salty and, no doubt, seamy side of Jamaican nature. But the ten-mile row across the harbor from Kingston to Port Henderson, over that iridescent sea, under a soft (to us) midsummer sun, the grand Blue Mountain scenery rising up into the clouds on our right, the long, low arm of Port Royal on our left, the wooded heights of Port Henderson in front, great pelicans soaring and diving obliquely into the water, all along the route, were not without their charm to me, especially as my companion did most of the pulling.

What made the old Scotch rhyme constantly hum itself in my mind, I do not know: —

" Little did my mither think the day she cradled me,
  The lands I was to travel in, the death I was to dee.''

Here we were in strange lands, indeed, but we had no fear of leaving our bones upon the sands of Great Salt Pond.

And surely the reception we met with at Port Henderson, at the hands of a family whose acquaintance we had previously made, does not belong to the tale of our woes, but of our joys. Such hospitality, — food, cheer, rest, — all so freely, gladly given, one would rarely find at home; but in Jamaica we found it everywhere. The generous human affections and impulses seem to grow as luxuriantly there as the vegetation. A pail of drinking-water was provided us here, as we should find none at Salt Pond, and in the early evening, the full moon flooding the sea and the land with its light, we set out for the pond, an hour's row distant, keeping under the abrupt, high, rocky shore, over a glassy sea, in the soft, luminous tropical night. Leisurely we rounded point after point, till the mountain ended and a low bushy shore was before us. In this, somewhere, was the narrow, almost hidden opening into Great Salt Pond. But the boy has a keen sense of topography ; he had been there once before by daylight ; so, with an instinct as unerring as that of some wild creature, the boat felt its way into the little gut or channel that connects the pond with the sea. In less than a hundred yards we emerged from the shadows of the verdure upon the still, moon-drenched, circular bit of land-locked sea. How weird and mystical it looked! a wild range of rocky, bushy hills upon one side, and low, wooded shores upon the other.

At the far side, a mile or more distant, standing upon the sand, was a small, dilapidated building used mainly by fishermen. To this point we directed our course, and in due time drew our boat up on the low, sandy beach.

The scene was wild and lonely in the extreme, but this was a part of what we had come for. We experienced our first disappointment when we found that the moonlight killed the phosphorescent display that we had hoped to see. Only a very pale blue flame could now be evoked from the water. My son's second disappointment came when his long and cautious promenade upon the shore, revolver in hand, and his long vigil by the inlet into a second salt pond revealed no crocodiles. In his absence I had scooped out a place in the sand, spread our blankets, and, with a couple of old doors raised over the spot to keep off the dews of the night, stretched myself out, a lodger for the first time with tropical nature. But sleep did not come easily; in fact, did not come at all. The ants from below and the mosquitoes from above soon found me out. The Jamaican sand ant is a subtle, persistent creature, and the mosquito is persistent without being subtle. Roll myself in my blanket and cover my face and head as I would, I could not shake off or discourage either. About midnight my son returned from his fruitless crocodile hunt, and joined me in the couch of sand. Youth can sleep, no matter what the conditions. Presently some strange water-fowl, whose hoarse honking and calling we had been hearing all the evening, spied us out there on the sand, and gathered about us; they stretched their necks, or, as the boys say, "rubbered" and "rubbered," and let off their weird notes of astonishment or alarm. In the moonlight I saw them standing at the water's edge and craning their necks, all alive with curiosity. Not till my son whipped out his revolver and fired at one of them did the disturbing, long-necked commenting upon our presence cease.

There in the stillness of the night we heard the wild cattle low in the woods beyond the marshes. (We had been told of a wild herd in this neighborhood.) Then mockingbirds, the Antillean species, sang in some near-by bushes, and the mosquitoes and ants still persisted. About two o'clock, finding sleep impossible, and that my body no longer fitted the mould in the sand, I shook myself out of my blanket and stepped forth, and instantly thanked my stars for my wakefulness, for there low in the southern horizon hung the Southern Cross, — four large, bright stars, one in each arm of the imaginary cross. I aroused my companion that he, too, might see this splendid spectacle of the southern heavens. It was the first and only view that we got during our stay on the island. This bit of new astronomy made me forget the pests of the sand. It was not long now till daylight, and something like an hour's sleep was snatched at the last moment. Before the sun was up I was washed and combed and listening to the vocal performances of the mockingbirds. It was not engaging music to me. I do not know how much this West Indian species falls short in musical ability of that of our own mockingbird of the Southern States, if any. But it was not a songster that I wished to take home with me as I did the solitaire. It was not equal to our catbird's song, and the morning carol of the robin would have made it seem cheap and trivial. It was bantering, hilarious, festive, but it had no sweetness, seriousness, or feeling.

We had our Primus stove with us *sans* alcohol, and my patience, even my temper, was sorely tried, and many matches were wasted, in trying to evoke with kerosene oil alone the intense blue flame that crowns success with this stove. But despite the wind, this feat was at last accomplished, and our breakfast of bacon, eggs, tea, and toast was achieved.

Then we rowed round the pond, and found the

narrow channel that joins it to the second pond. Into this we made our way, and discovered that it was semi-stagnant. It was a likely place for crocodiles, but we saw none, — only a large, heron-like water-fowl that was suspicious of our approach.

The most striking scene here was a kind of vegetable Hades where we landed and tarried a short time. If the bad spirits in the vegetable world go to a bad place, this is probably where they bring up; or, as I said to my son, if the human imps — mean-ness, spitefulness, jealousy, uncharitableness, and backbiting — were to take vegetable form, here we doubtless see what they would be like, — a thick, rank growth of several forms of cacti, intermingled with various thorned and fanged bushes standing upon a jagged, crabbed, deeply seamed rocky floor. Under the hot sun the place exhaled a peculiarly disagreeable odor. With great difficulty I pushed my way into it a few yards. If there had only been a few writhing, hissing serpents there and a horned toad or two, the scene would have been complete. Some of the fluted, cylindrical growths of cacti towered up twenty feet, and were so thickly set with rows of long, sharp, vicious needles that it fairly made the eyes water to look at them. This was the fanged side of tropical nature, and we soon had enough of it. These huge growths of cacti were fleshy and tender like fruit; one could hack into them with his knife as into a melon or an apple, but what eats them? Why all this terrible panoply of spines? The spine and the thorn everywhere, I suppose, is simply a sign of savage, unregenerate nature. We saw in Jamaica some species of palm, so bristling with long, awl-like thorns that one could not look at them without a positive feeling of discomfort. Think of the amount of original sin there must be in such a tree! And no fruit to guard, either, — just a spontaneous overflow of the hatred and spitefulness of the old fire-eating, all-devouring, seismic earth!

Great Salt Pond is shallow, of a uniform depth of about three and a half feet, so that the fishermen wade in, hauling their nets. The evaporation is so great that the water seems to be always flowing in from the sea.

On our way out we found a boat at the inlet with our friends the Davises, — a father and three sons, — from Port Henderson. Their hospitality and solicitude for our well-being had brought them the four miles with a pail of fresh water. In the inlet, which was running like a mill race, we all went in bathing, partly for a bath, but chiefly of necessity to haul and push our boats out against the current. How delicious that bath was, except that the savage current hurled both my son and me against the banks with such force that our skins were gashed in several places.

Here we saw that large, beautiful tropical fish, the

" calipeever," darting about or poising in the swiftly running, transparent water, as large as a salmon trout.

Then came the quiet afternoon row back to Kingston, with more refreshment and cheer at the house of our Port Henderson friends, the superb Blue Mountain scenery on the one hand, and Port Royal and the open sea on the other.

The birds in Jamaican waters that amused us most were the great, ill-shaped, lubberly pelicans. Everywhere in the bays and harbors we would see them poising and diving. From a hundred feet or so above the water, they hurl themselves down recklessly, striking the surface with a great splash. But they usually get the fish. My son aptly described their flight as that of a bird sitting down to fly. Most water-fowl fly with head and neck stretched straight out, but the pelican draws his head back, curves his neck, and seems to sit down upon his great hulk of a body and row himself along with his huge wings.

Kingston we found a dull, hot, uninviting place, — low houses, dirty streets, with a colored population, for the most part ragged and lazy. It is a city of crowing roosters. They begin at nine o'clock promptly, and crow every hour, if not oftener, the night through. When one gives the signal, you hear the challenge taken up all about, the chorus swelling and spreading till a wave of shrill-voiced sound sweeps over the city. Then another wave, and another, three or four times repeated, till they finally die down, to remain so till the hour strikes again. The traveler tarrying in Kingston soon comes to wish that the mongoose had made poultry-raising still more difficult than it is.

And the dogs were not far behind the roosters. But the flea and the tick do not leave much spirit in the Jamaican dog. Poor cur, how wretched and forlorn he looks ! That he can bark at all is a wonder. And it is only in town that he does bark, and in the cool of the night. In the country he looks at you wistfully, or languidly searches his own body for the pests that make his life miserable.

Everywhere the cocoanut-trees are upon the beach or near it. There seems to be a fringe of them around the whole island. They lean toward the sea as if they loved it ; or does this attitude enable them the better to withstand the gales from the sea ? We saw them upon small islands, — in one case a solitary tree upon a little coral reef a few yards in extent, still yearning seaward. The wind blows back their long leaves so that they suggest runners with their hair streaming behind them.

The palms of all sorts seem less like trees than like gigantic woody plants. They have no branches, — only a stalk with a tuft of leaves at the top. The wood is not wood, but bundles of tough fibres like cords and ropes ; and the leaves are not leaves, but more fibres welded together in tin-like sheets and

A Jamaica Family at Home

spears that rattle in the wind. They curve and sway gracefully, but it is rather the grace and neatness of geometric figures than of wild free growths. The roots, too, are not roots like those of other trees, but mops of cords of a uniform size. The cocoanut-tree lays hold of the ground by ten thousand of these cords about the size of a pipe-stem, which in the stem are gathered together and welded into a huge cable, eight or ten inches through. The growth of the cocoanut is in but one direction, — upward. The stem does not increase in size as it shoots heavenward. A tree sixty feet high has a trunk no larger than one ten feet high. Up, up it goes, like some extension arrangement or appliance, perpetually pushing out new leaves and new fruit blossoms at the top, and dropping the old ones; always with a circle of ripened fruit surmounted by other circles of half-grown and just formed nuts, crowned by a ring of new, cream-colored bloom. Its young leaves emerge from the parent stem swathed in coarse burlap. Their swaddling-clothes would make a shirt in which the most austere and fanatical of the old monks might have done penance. Probably nothing else is born in the world wrapped up in such a harsh, forbidding integument; a product of the tree's interior juices and vital functions, it is nevertheless as dry and stiff and apparently as lifeless as the product of a weaver's loom. Its office seems to be to hold up and to protect the young leaf till it can stand and wave alone. Then it begins to let go and peel away. From one young tree I cut enough of this natural hemp cloth to make me a shirt, should I be seized with the penitential fit. It possesses regular warp and woof, and the fibres are crossed over and under as in real cloth. The cocoanut is strongly expressive of one side of tropical nature, — its hard, harsh, glittering, barbaric side.

To our northern eyes, Nature in the tropics has little tenderness or winsomeness. She is barbaric; she is painty and stiff; she has no sentiment; she does not touch the heart; she flouts and revels and goes her own way like a wanton. She has never known adversity; she has no memory and no longing; there is no autumn behind her and no spring before; she is a prodigal, she lives in the present, she runs to spikes and spines; perpetual summer has given her the hue and tone of August, — dark, strident, cloying. She is rank, she is wicked; she stings and stabs and bites you, or she heeds you not. No turf in the fields, no carpet of moss and lichens in the woods. Indeed, the woods are barred against you. It is impossible to make your way into them without cutting a path. The tangle of vines, the spiny growths, the interlocked branches, the close and fierce and unending struggle for existence of all manner of plants, bushes, and trees, make walking in the woods out of the question.

Only where the superb roads and bridle-paths lay them open, can you thread their interiors. And there you walk between walls of rank vegetation, — no glimpses along forest aisles and corridors, no long, cool perspectives, no leaf-strewn floors of checkered sunlight and shadow, no interior housed and cloistered effects at all. Apparently the woods in Jamaica are never swept by fire any more than they are in Alaska; the dense ground vegetation and the humidity secure them against the besom of the flames. The trees cast their leaves one by one, apparently, the year through, like the human tree: always falling leaves, always new buds and blossoms. We saw wild blackberries (poor things), with ripe fruit and green, and just opened blossoms. The word sylvan belongs to higher latitudes. There are lairs and jungles and smothering dungeons in tropical forests, but no clean, restful sylvan solitude.

How much the beauty of our northern landscape owes to grass, — this green nap or pile of the fields and hills, so tender, so uniform, so humanizing, softening the outlines, tempering the light, loving the snow and the moisture, bringing out the folds and dimples of plain and slope, and clothing the northern mountains as with veils of green gauze! The tropical grasses are coarse, broad-leafed, — crab grass, Bahama grass, Guinea grass, — good forage, but not pleasing to look upon, and the landscape is but slightly affected by them.

FAR AND NEAR

I cannot conceive of any poetry ever being produced in the tropics. Nature and life there do not make the poetic appeal. There is little that is heroic, or plaintive, or pathetic, or that stimulates the imagination or fosters sentiment. The beak and claw and spine and thorn side of nature is more pronounced than in our zone ; forms are more savage, disease is more deadly. Man cannot take Nature to himself and dominate and tame and humanize her, as he can where snow falls and spring comes. Nature moulds and stamps him, and develops his fangs of passion.

How much our civilization owes to the winter and to the spring! to the tender, to the heroic, to the prophetic moods of Nature. How are our lives enriched and deepened and stimulated by the changes of the seasons : the spring with its yearning and allurements, the summer with its victories and defeats, the autumn with its repose and plenty, the winter with its spur and tonic, — what would our lives be without these things?

The leaves of the trees in Jamaica are for the most part thick and stiff and shining, — varnished by the sun and the heat. The foliage rarely presents the airy, feathery, graceful character of the foliage of our trees. The landscape is rarely impressive. It is deficient in the elements of simplicity and dignity. It is too often a jumble of broken and insignificant lines. It was not moulded

264

and sculptured by the old ice gods in late geologic times as ours was. It looks crude and unfinished to northern eyes, like certain of our Rocky Mountain views. In the Blue Mountains, however, one gets glimpses of the long, sweeping, masterful lines that are characteristic of our mountain scenery. The higher parts of the mountains are in the grand style. They suggest the Catskills, but are steeper and loftier by several hundred feet, Blue Mountain Peak reaching an altitude of seventy-three hundred feet. Their backs are not so broad as those of the Catskills; they have not been worn down in the same way. They are wooded to their summits. One of our most delightful experiences was the week we spent upon them at New Castle, four thousand feet above the sea.

Jamaica is poor in animal life. No squirrels, nor foxes, nor rabbits, nor marmots, nor bears, nor deer in the woods, — no four-footed game at all, and only a short list of native birds. We met a few of our own summer residents there spending the winter, — the Maryland yellow-throat, the black and white creeping warbler, the redstart. In one place on the edge of some woods I saw the oven-bird walking about in its pretty, contented way as at home, and along the mountain streams I heard the sharp *chip* of the water-wagtail, as along my own streams. None of these birds were in song, and probably in early March they turned their faces northward, no doubt making their first flight of ninety miles to Cuba, then continuing by way of the Bahamas to the Florida coast.

I heard but one bird in the island that touched my heart, and that was the solitaire, a thrush-like bird that belongs to the genus *Myadestes*. It is colored like our catbird, and of about the same size. It has a white mark near the eye ; hence the natives call it "shine eye." It is very shy and secluded in its habits, and is often known as the invisible bird. I heard it hundreds of times, but saw it only twice. It is found only in the mountains after an altitude of two or three thousand feet is attained. I have never heard a bird-note more expressive of seclusion and wild solitude, — melodious, plaintive, far-heard, it sounds through the twilight forests like a call to some holy rite or festival. It made me think of Keats's "Ode to a Nightingale;" it has the same magic quality, the power of pure music to call up visions of "faery lands forlorn."

" Forlorn ; the very word is like a bell,''

and there was something bell-like in the "plaintive anthem" of this bird. It usually began with a series of tinkling, bell-like notes, — from a golden bell, if that were possible. These were followed by two long, tapering, flute-like strains in different keys, exquisitely melodious and appealing. It was a voice

from out the heart of sacred solitude, and made
me want to follow

"And with thee fade away into the forest dim:

"Fade far away, dissolve, and quite forget
What thou among the leaves hast never known,
The weariness, the fever, and the fret
Here, where men sit and hear each other groan."

When I first heard a single bar of the song, I was
strongly reminded of the plaint of the Oregon robin
as I had heard it in the wilds of Alaska. It was the
same tapering, soulful monotone. This may be the
reason that the full song seemed to me more expressive of Alaskan solitudes, with so much in them that
was to the eye what pure melody is to the ear, than
of tropical forests.

There is another bird in Jamaica (called by the
natives the Spanish quail, because there is a look
about the head that suggests the quail), that I heard
briefly on one occasion utter notes much like those
of the solitaire. The native oriole has a whistle that
recalls that of our oriole, and the native kingbird
is almost a copy of ours. A species of grackle or
crow blackbird, with his white eye, had a very familiar look. A queer, clownish-looking bird is the little
tody, with its green suit and large, golden beak. It
looked as if made up for some carnival. I did not
hear it sing or rehearse its part. There are several

small birds called "quits," as the blue quit, the grass quit, the orange quit. We found a nest of the last-named bird on the limb of an orange-tree, a curious structure woven of fine grasses, and shaped like a gourd with the neck bent over the limb, so that the entrance was upon one side of the branch and the body of the nest upon the other. The latter part of February the grass quit was building a nest in a climbing vine over the door of the house where we were staying. The male seemed more industrious in carrying sticks and straws than the female, — praise I had never before known a male bird to deserve. The song was fine and insect-like.

Three species of hummingbirds were noticeable. One large one, called the "doctor," nearly black, with two long plumes in its tail, drew our attention frequently. When it flew, these long, narrow plumes trailed or undulated behind it, producing a curious rocket-like effect, or the effect of some ingenious toy. In the mountains I saw the black mango hummingbird gathering spiders' webs from the rocks, no doubt to be used in sticking the lichens upon the nest, after the manner of our ruby-throat.

Mockingbirds were common throughout the island, — the Antillean form appearing almost identical with our southern mockingbird. The mating season was at hand, and the birds were full of action and of song; the latter quite unmusical, never as pleasing as that of our catbird.

A LOST FEBRUARY

The only wild animal that we saw in Jamaica was the mongoose, and this was not often seen. We had glimpses of three or four, during our month's stay on the island, hurriedly crossing the road in front of us, or darting into the bushes. They suggested a large weasel or a light-colored mink. They are very destructive to everything that lives and nests upon the ground. They have even driven the rats into the trees ; we saw several rats' nests amid the branches. They make eggs and poultry expensive on account of their depredations upon the hencoops.

Our last week in Jamaica was spent at Bowden on Port Morant, near the extreme eastern end of the island. Bowden proved to be the most restful and enjoyable place we had found — a most delightful change from the heat, dust, and squalor of Kingston. The hotel, called Peak View Cottages, owned by the United Fruit Company, is situated on a ridge three hundred feet above the harbor, with the sea on one hand and the huge pile of the Blue Mountains on the other. A fresh breeze was always blowing, the Caribbean Sea was always full of delicate, shifting rainbow tints, the ten thousand cocoanut palms that covered hill and valley about us were always rustling and swaying, and the Blue Mountains and the John Crow range, with a vast stretch of wooded country between us and them, with plantation houses at intervals gleaming out of the dank green,

were there to draw and delight the eye with the
rugged and the sublime. We could see the steamers far at sea, coming round the point of the island
and making for our harbor. Late one afternoon
I watched a steamer leaving for South Africa, slanting slowly away from the island into the Caribbean
and fading from view, — going down behind the
rim of the great ocean-girdled world. What a speck,
creeping slowly down and around, over the shining
surface of the great sphere toward that far-off land!

Here, where we only expected to stop over night
on our way to Manchioneal, we tarried for a week,
and gave ourselves up to the mood or the whim
of the moment, sitting for hours on the cottage
porches, gazing upon the strange scenes, drinking
in tropical nature through all our senses, our
eyes following the calmly, majestically sailing turkey buzzards that were everywhere in evidence,
then resting on the long line of cocoanut palms
where the surf was breaking upon the coral reefs
two miles away. Glancing over the broad sweep of
palms near at hand, rustling and glinting in the sun,
our eyes plunged down into the green waters of the
bay below us on the west, then darted away to the
mountains where Cuna Cuna Pass invited us to
continue our journey to Manchioneal, or alighted on
the changing cloud drapery that hid Blue Mountain Peak.

One day we took a leisurely drive to the Hot

Springs at Bath and gathered our first nutmegs and Otahitu apples. Day after day we made our way down through palm groves, past trees and bushes, to the beach, where we bathed in the warm surf, cut our feet upon the coral rocks, sat upon or examined the rusty, time-eaten cannon that had lain exposed or half buried in the ruined fortifications for more than a hundred years, contemplated the strange and curious forms of vegetable life, or watched the pelicans diving, and the fiddler crabs " scrapping " upon the shore. We talked with the people at their cabin doors and watched the men taking the husks from the cocoanuts as the women gathered them; we loitered upon the dock and watched the girls and women loading the fruit steamers with bananas — an endless chain of women and girls going from the little cars to the steamer's side, all bearing bunches of bananas on their heads, often continuing the work till past midnight, and toward the last, when tired and sleepy, timing their movements to a wild musical chant. They were all barefoot and rather ragged and soiled, the dripping of the juice from the freshly cut banana stems soon besmearing their clothes. Thirty thousand bunches of the fruit were thus often put on the steamer in a single night. The women earned about eighteen pence each.

One day we made an excursion on the little toy-like railway out to Golden Grove, six or eight miles distant, in the last century a large sugar plantation, now a banana and cocoanut plantation owned by the United Fruit Company. The little railway connected the plantation with the steamer. Train-loads of bananas and cocoanuts were brought in to the steamers daily. Golden Grove is a large, oval, fertile plain, threaded by the limpid Gardner River and surrounded by an amphitheatre of hills and mountains. Most of the large, solid, whitewashed buildings of the old sugar plantation were still standing; some of them with the high-arched bridge were very picturesque. Here we saw many East Indian coolies, — a slight, slender, sooty-faced race, the women often in rags, with silver bands on their ankles and wrists. Here, too, we saw a large herd of East Indian oxen, — wide-horned, high-shouldered, dewlapped creatures, with a wonderful look of dignity and repose. A coolie woman, stripped to the waist, was washing her clothes in the river near the ruins of the old mill, while her little girl of ten or twelve was bathing in the pool near by. It was a pretty picture, and my son determined to get a photograph of it. When the woman saw what he was about she was very indignant and voluble, but she was too late; the camera winks quickly. A few pennies would have made her a willing subject.

For some reason, before I went to Jamaica I had thought of the banana as growing upon a tree, but here it was growing upon a kind of huge cornstalk,

— a stalk the size of one's leg and fifteen or twenty feet high, — one bunch of fruit from each stalk or plant. When the fruit is gathered the old stalk is cut away, and a new sprout from the root takes its place. The stalk is composed of the stems of the big long leaves. The bunch of bananas springs directly out of the heart of the plant. There is nothing superficial or fortuitous about it as there is with most fruit. It is the whole show; it is a serious matter; it sums up the whole plant. One can see where the bud is before it emerges, by the swelling of the stalk, — like the bird or frog in the snake's body.

I doubt if there is any future for Jamaica. It seems to me it is bound to remain pretty much as it now is. Its black population have not the seeds of progress. The resources of the island are not great except in the production of fruit, and for this there is no free market near at hand. There is no mineral wealth, and no tempting field for capital. For the past ten years its imports have exceeded its exports by a million dollars annually. This difference is probably made good by tourists from this country and from England. American capital and American enterprise are doing more for the island than are British. Banana culture, already on a large scale, is increasing, and is mainly the work of the United Fruit Company.

The burden of taxation in the island is excessive,

and kills all native enterprise. If a new industry starts, it is taxed out of existence. I was told of several that had been thus killed. They literally tax the wheels off the wagons, the tax being about five dollars a wheel. A man is afraid to make any improvement about his house, — to add another window, or to put on a piazza or a new roof, — lest his taxes be increased. I heard of an American who took an automobile there to make a tour of the island, but the sum demanded by the authorities before they would allow him to land it — something over a hundred dollars — was so great that he went back home with it on the steamer's return trip.

Hence I say that the tax-gatherer is the incubus that weighs down Jamaica. The people are excessively taxed, largely to pay big salaries to the tax-gatherers. The governor, quite a useless personage, it seems to me, is paid five thousand pounds a year, and there is a long string of office-holders below him, grading down to the police commissioners, that all draw big pay. Imports are taxed. Every family that buys a barrel of flour pays two dollars to the government.

The roads and bridle-paths in Jamaica symbolize England; they are England clasping the island as with a many-fingered hand. You walk or ride along these superb imperial highways and look out upon a land semi-savage; civilization under foot, and barbarism just across the fence, — little or no agri-

274

culture or fruit culture, or culture of any kind as we understand the word, except where the great Fruit Companies have possession; the landscape marred and torn, but not subdued; no open fields, no smooth hill-slopes, rarely a well-kept garden or a bit of lawn; rude fertile nature everywhere, struggling to shake off the lazy grasp of these black children. Lazy they no doubt are. During the three or four months of the mango season, we were told, it is very difficult to get man or woman to work. As the mangoes grow everywhere, the people subsist upon them, and life becomes a holiday. Hence the fruit companies and sugar planters have to import coolie labor, East Indiamen, — a feeble race, but faithful and reliable. We saw a great gathering of these people in Kingston living in a large warehouse on one of the docks. They had worked out their ten years, and were awaiting a steamer to take them back to India. How homesick many of them were, poor souls, and how tedious the waiting was to them! They were a quiet, picturesque crowd, but very wary of the camera, unless we first sprinkled them with a little copper. When we were sauntering through the market, the Indian women, crouched by their baskets filled with stuff on sale, would spring up and turn their backs the moment they saw the camera in my son's hand. They seem a much prouder and more exclusive race than the African.

FAR AND NEAR

Just now I called the negro lazy, though that is probably not strictly the right word. The negro in Jamaica is childish, immature, void of any serious purpose in life, rather than lazy. He is haunted by no ideals : sufficient for the day are the mangoes thereof, and why should he fret and struggle ? Those women forever upon the road, making long marches with their burdens, were not lazy; they were children that took life lightly and carelessly.

The price of labor is low in Jamaica, yet anything is dear that costs more than it is worth, and much of the low-priced labor is expensive. On one of the plantations of the United Fruit Company I saw a coolie cleaning the ground of grass and weeds in an orange orchard with a big long-handled hoe at a rate for a given area that was more than four times the price I could have done it for with a horse and cultivator. A vast deal of hand-work is done where we use horses and machinery.

Most of the road-making and road-mending seems done by women and girls. They are the real beasts of burden. They break up the stone and carry it in bags upon their heads and dump it down where it is wanted. One day I sat half an hour upon the bank by the roadside, and got myself covered with ticks, watching a woman raking the broken stone in place, while my companion was photographing a big cottonwood-tree.

We left Jamaica on the return trip the 3d of March, just about the time I fancy that the birds from our woods that we had met there were also turning their faces northward. We reached home on the 9th, and at sundown the caroling of the robins from the treetops was far more welcome than any bird voice we heard in Jamaica, not even excepting that of the solitaire.

INDEX

INDEX

Bomb Point, 79.
Boneset, climbing, 209.
Boneset, purple, 209.
Boneset, white, 209.
Bougainvillea, 229.
Bowden, Jamaica, 269–271.
Boy, a winsome colored, 233.
Brady, John Green, Governor of Alaska, 54.
Brewer, Prof. William H., 22, 65, 92.
Bryanthus, 68.
Bryn Mawr Glacier, 73.
Bunting, hyperborean snow, *or* McKay's snowflake (*Passerina nivalis hyperborea*), 120; song of, 120; nest of, 123.
Bunting, indigo. *See* Indigo-bird.
Bunting, lark (*Calamospiza melanocorys*), 4.
Bunting, snow, *or* snowflake (*Passerina nivalis*), a part of the winter, 180; a flock of, 180, 181; attacked by hawks and shrikes, 180, 181; 189; notes of, 180.
Bunting, snow, *or* Pribilof snowflake (*Passerina nivalis townsendi*), 101, 106.
Buttercup, 251.
Buzzard, turkey, *or* turkey vulture (*Cathartes aura*), 227, 270.

Cacti, 257.
Calipeever, 259.
Camping-out, in Jamaica, 252–259.
Campion, moss, 52, 53.
Canyons, 7, 12–14, 17.
Cape Fox, 127.
Cape Nome, 113.
Cardinal-flower, 152, 153, 214.
Cassiope, 88.
Cattle, wild, 255.
Caves, in Jamaica, 246, 247.
Cawein, Madison J., quotation from, 211, 212.
Cedar-bird, *or* cedar waxwing (*Ampelis cedrorum*), 176.
Chapelton, Jamaica, 232, 237–239.
Chasm, a, 122.
Chickadee (*Parus atricapillus*), a

sitting bird, 137, 138; checks to the increase of, 138, 139; 167, 173, 174, 176, 177, 183–185; sleeping-places of, 188, 189; nest of, 136, 137, 215.
Chickadee, rufous - backed, *or* chestnut-backed chickadee (*Parus rufescens*), 33, 55, 128.
Chickweed, 121.
Chipmunk, 154.
Chippy. *See* Sparrow, social.
Clarence Straits, 31, 32.
Clarkia, 17.
Claytonia, 114, 121.
Clematis, wild, 210.
Clover, white, 251.
Cobwebs, 209.
Cock Pit country, Jamaica, 243, 246, 247.
Cocoanuts, 271.
Cocoanut-trees, 260–262.
Coffee, pounding, 232.
Coleyville, Jamaica, 244–246.
Collector, a human weasel, 155.
Columbia Glacier, 71.
Columbia River, journey along, 18–20.
Columbine, in Alaska, 64.
Cook Inlet, 80, 81, 125.
Coolies, East Indian, in Jamaica, 272, 275.
Coon, 154.
Cormorant (*Phalacrocorax* sp.), 119.
Cottonwood, 233.
Coville, Frederick V., 22, 65.
Cowbird (*Molothrus ater*), notes of, 151.
Cowcatcher, riding on the, 8, 9.
Coyote, 4, 11.
Creeper, brown (*Certhia familiaris americana*), 174.
Cricket. *See* Tree-cricket.
Crocodile, 252.
Crow, American (*Corvus brachyrhynchos*), 157.
Crow, fish (*Corvus ossifragus*), 158.

Daisy, ox-eye, 201.
Dall, Dr. William H., 22, 65.
Davidson Glacier, 35.

280

INDEX

Dead Horse Trail, 37.
Deer, 25–27.
Dellenbaugh, Fred S., 22.
Devereux, W. B., 22, 65.
Devil's club, 28.
Devil's Thumb, 33.
Dipper, American. *See* Ouzel, water.
Dogs, in Jamaica, 232, 260.
Doran, Capt. Peter, 65, 75.
Douglas Island, 34.
Dove, mourning (*Zenaidura macroura*), 9.
Duck, eider (*Somateria* sp.), 111.
Ducks, wild, and gunners, 148–150.
Duncan, Rev. William, 29, 30.
Dutch Harbor, 98–101, 124.

Eagle, bald (*Haliæetus leucocephalus*), 24, 25; inspiration of the presence of, 154–156; and the collector, 155; 161.
Eagles, 34.
Eider. *See* Duck, eider.
Elk Mountains, the, 5.
Elliot, Daniel G., 22, 76.
Emerson, Prof. Benjamin K., 22, 66, 108.
Eskimos, 72; an encampment in Siberia, 108–111; at Port Clarence, 112, 113; villages ruined by whiskey, 118.
Etolin Island, 32.
Ewarton, Jamaica, 231, 232.

Fairweather Range, 53, 56, 57, 126.
Farms, in the East and in the West, 2, 3.
Fernow, Dr. B. E., 22.
Ferns, tree, 250.
Finch, house (*Carpodacus mexicanus frontalis*), 15.
Finch, rosy, or Hepburn's leucosticte (*Leucosticte tephrocotis littoralis*), 38, 52, 94, 123.
Fireflies, Jamaican, 238.
Fish, flying-fish, 224, 225; mullet, 241; calipeever, 259.
Fisher, Dr. A. K., 22.

Flicker, northwestern. *See* Highhole, western.
Flowers, on the plains, 11; on Kadiak Island, 88; at Plover Bay, 111; of the tundra at Port Clarence, 114; on Hall and St. Matthew Islands, 121, 122; on Black Creek, 152, 153; of August, 202–204, 209, 210; on Katherine's Peak, Jamaica, 251.
Flycatcher, Arkansas, *or* Arkansas kingbird (*Tyrannus verticalis*), 15.
Flyeatcher, great crested (*Myiarchus crinitus*), 138.
Flying-fish, 224, 225.
Forest, a buried, 50.
Foresting, Nature's manner of, 45.
Forget-me-not, 88, 111.
Fort Wrangell, 32, 33.
Fox, blue, 71, 124, 125.
Fox, Hall Island arctic, 123.
Fox, red, 154.
Fox, silver-black, 125.
Fox farms, 71, 72, 124, 125.
Frankfield, Jamaica, 239, 242.
Frederick Sound, 33.
Fringed-orchis, small purple, 204.
Fuertes, Louis Agassiz, 66.
Fulmar, Pacific (*Fulmarus glacialis glupischa*), 124.
Fungi. *See* Mushrooms.

Gannett, Henry, 22, 62, 76, 80.
Gardner River, 272.
George W. Elder, the steamer, 20, 21; breaks propeller, 75; caught in a strong tide, 77; mending her propeller, 77, 78; strikes a rock, 107.
Geranium, wild, at Kadiak, 88.
Gerardia, rose, 203.
Gifford, R. Swain, 125.
Gilbert, G. K., 22, 44, 62, 65.
Ginger farming, 243, 244.
Girl, a little, mistakes the author for Santa Claus, 226, 227.
Glacier Bay, 39, 44.
Glaciers, 35, 53, 57, 82; Patterson, 33; Davidson, 35; Muir, 39–53;

INDEX

Morse, 49, 59 ; Malaspina, 58, 66, 67 ; Turner, 59; Hubbard, 59, 62; on mountain precipices, 60, 61, 73; Hidden, 62 ; Nunatak, 62 ; Columbia, 71; on Port Wells, 73, 74; Barry, 75, 77 ; on Harriman Fiord, 76, 77 ; Serpentine, 76 ; Stairway, 76 ; Harriman, 77.

Golden Grove, Jamaica, 271, 272.

Goldfinch, American (*Astragalinus tristis*), in winter, 179; the bird of August, 207; notes of, 179 ; nest and eggs of, 207, 208.

Gold-seekers, privations of, 68–70; returning, 124.

Good, John, 241, 242.

Gorse, in Jamaica, 251.

Grackle (*Quiscalus crassirostris*), of Jamaica, 267.

Grackle, rusty, *or* rusty blackbird (*Euphagus carolinus*), notes of, 150.

Graham Reach, 26.

Grass, in the northern landscape and in the tropics, 263.

Great Salt Pond, 252–258.

Green River, 7.

Grenville Channel, 128.

Grinnell, Dr. George Bird, 22, 66.

Grosbeak, Kadiak pine (*Pinicola enucleator flammula*), 64, 89.

Grouse, ruffed (*Bonasa umbellus*), 189.

Gulls, 75, 119.

Gunning for ducks, 148–150.

Gustavus Peninsula, 44, 45.

Haenke Island, 63.

Hall Island, 118–121.

Hares, 12.

Harriman, Edward H., 1, 10, 21, 65, 75, 76 ; kills a Kadiak bear, 90, 91 ; 107–109.

Harriman Alaska Expedition, 1–129; its composition, 1; its outfit and personnel, 21, 22 ; social life and entertainments of, 65, 66; celebrates the Fourth of July, 92.

Harriman Fiord, 75–77, 80.

Harriman Glacier 77.

Harvard Glacier, 73.

Hawk, broad-winged (*Buteo platypterus*), cry of, 158, 159; nest and young of, 158, 159.

Hawk, Cooper's (*Accipiter cooperii*), 158.

Hawk, duck (*Falco peregrinus anatum*), 158.

Hawk, red-tailed (*Buteo borealis*), 157, 251.

Hawk, sharp-shinned (*Accipiter velox*), 158.

Hawk, sparrow (*Falco sparverius*), 158.

Hawks, 9, 157, 158; in August, 208, 209.

Hawkweed, orange-colored, 202.

Hector's River, 246.

Heron, green (*Butorides virescens*), 237.

Hidden Glacier, 62.

Highhole, western, *or* northwestern flicker (*Colaptes cafer saturatior*), 23.

Hix, Colonel, 243.

Howling Valley, 43, 44.

Hubbard Glacier, 59, 62.

Hudson River, a house by, 131, 132; algæ in, 210, 211; August on, 213, 214.

Hummingbird, long - tailed, *or* " doctor " (*Aithurus polytmus*), 268.

Hummingbird, mango (*Lampornis mango*), 268.

Hummingbird, rufous (*Selasphorus rufus*), 128.

Iliuliuk, 98.

Indian Point, 112.

Indian River, 55.

Indians, Alaskan, 28; at Metlakahtla, 29, 30; characteristics of, 30, 31; an encampment of, 63, 64; summer life of, 63, 64; a deserted village of, 127.

Indigo-bird, *or* indigo bunting (*Cyanospiza cyanea*), song of, 205.

Iris, 88.

INDEX

Irrigation, 15.
Isanotski Volcano, 97, 98.

Jacob's ladder, 88.
Jaeger (*Stercorarius* sp.), 64, 121.
Jamaica, visit to, 223–277 ; a country cursed with perpetual summer, 223; arrival at, 226; roadsides in, 228, 229; streams in, 230–232; roads in, 233, 274; stars in, 249, 256 ; hospitality in, 253 ; woods in, 262, 263; grasses in, 263; leaves of the trees in, 264; the landscape in, 264, 265; mammals of, 265, 269; birds of, 265–268 ; future of, 273 ; taxation in, 273, 274; agriculture in, 274, 275; labor in, 275, 276 ; road-making in, 276 ; return from, 277. *See also* Negroes, Jamaican.
Jay, blue (*Cyanocitta cristata*), thieving propensity of, 166, 167; 183–185.
Jay, Steller's (*Cyanocitta stelleri*), 33, 128.
John Crow Mountains, 269.
Joseph, a colored servant, 248.
Judas Vale, Jamaica, 236, 237.
Junco, Oregon (*Junco hyemalis oreganus*), 33, 45.
Juneau, 34, 126.

Kachemac Bay, 80.
Kadiak, the village, 85–87, 124.
Kadiak Island, 81–92, 124.
Katherine's Peak, 248–251.
Katydid, 208.
Keeler, Charles A., 66, 91, 92.
Kelly, Captain, 64.
Kendal, Jamaica, 243.
Kingbird, gray (*Tyrannus dominicensis*), 267.
Kinglet, golden-crowned (*Regulus satrapa*), 174, 178, 183, 184.
Kinglet, golden-crowned (*Regulus satrapa* subsp.), 45, 55, 128.
Kinglet, ruby-crowned (*Regulus calendula*), rivalries of the males, 178, 179.
Kinglet, ruby-crowned (*Regulus calendula* subsp.), 45.

Kingston, a winter day in, 227, 228; 231, 247; seen from Katherine's Peak, 248 ; 252; a dull, hot, uninviting place, 259 ; the roosters of, 259, 260 ; the dogs of, 260; 275.
Kling-kling, 230.
Kondakoff, Stepan, 91.
Kukak Bay, 82, 93.

Lady's-slipper, at Kadiak, 88.
Lady's - tresses (*Spiranthes cernua*), 204.
Laramie plains, the, 5.
Lark, horned (*Otocoris alpestris* subsp.), 4, 9, 12.
Lark, prairie horned (*Otocoris alpestris praticola*), 165, 166.
Larkspur, 11.
Leucosticte, Hepburn's. *See* Finch, rosy.
Lice, grass, 229, 230.
Lizards, in Jamaica, 228.
Locomotive, riding on, 8, 9.
Logwood, 233.
Long Island, near Kadiak, 124, 125.
Longspur, Lapland, *or* Alaska longspur (*Calcarius lapponicus alascensis*), 98, 99 ; verses addressed to, 99; 106, 111, 115; song of, 98, 99, 120.
Loosestrife, purple, 152, 153, 209, 210.
Lowe Inlet, 27.
Lupine, 11, 16, 64, 88.
Lynn Canal, 35.

Machete, the ubiquitous, 249, 250.
Magpie, black-billed (*Pica pica hudsonia*), 16, 85, 125.
Malaspina Glacier, 58, 66, 67.
Meadow-beauty, *or* rhexia, 202.
Meadowlark, western (*Sturnella magna neglecta*), 12 ; song of, 4.
Merriam, Dr. C. Hart, 22.
Metlakahtla, 29–31.
Middleton Island, 67.
Milbank Sound, 26.
Milkweed, swamp, 209.
Mill, an old sugar, 242.

283

INDEX

INDEX

INDEX

INDEX